SAINSBURY'S

PASTA

JENI WRIGHT

ACKNOWLEDGEMENTS

Series Editor: **Nicola Hill**
Editor: **Lesley McOwan**
Copy Editor: **Suzy Powling**
Art Editor: **Lisa Tai**
Designer: **Sue Storey**
Production Controller: **Alyssum Ross**
Photographer: **James Murphy**
Home Economist: **Allyson Birch**
Stylists: **Carolyn Russell** and **Sarah Wiley**
Jacket Photographer: **Vernon Morgan**
Jacket Home Economist: **Allyson Birch**
Jacket Stylist: **Lorrie Mack**

NOTES

1. Standard level spoon measurements are used in all recipes.
1 tablespoon = one 15ml spoon
1 teaspoon = one 5ml spoon

2. Both metric and imperial measurements have been given in all recipes. Use one set of measurements only and not a mixture of both.

3. Ovens should be preheated to the specified temperature – if using a fan assisted oven, follow manufacturer's instructions for adjusting the temperature.

4. Eggs should be size 3 unless otherwise stated.

5. Pepper should be freshly ground black pepper unless otherwise stated.

6. Milk should be full-fat unless otherwise stated.

7. Fresh herbs should be used unless otherwise stated. If unavailable use dried herbs as an alternative but halve the quantities stated.

8. All microwave information is based on a 650 watt oven. Follow manufacturer's instructions for an oven with a different wattage.

Published exclusively for
J Sainsbury plc
Stamford Street, London SE1 9LL
by Cathay Books, an imprint of Reed Consumer Books Limited
Michelin House, 81 Fulham Road, London SW3 6RB
and Auckland, Melbourne, Singapore and Toronto

First published 1989
Reprinted 1991, 1992, 1993

ISBN 0 86178 526 6

Produced by Mandarin Offset
Printed in Hong Kong

CONTENTS

INTRODUCTION

PASTA IS GOOD FOR YOU! AND CONTRARY TO POPULAR BELIEF IT IS *NOT* FATTENING. IT IS LOW IN FAT, RICH IN CARBOHYDRATE AND A VALUABLE SOURCE OF ENERGY. EXTREMELY VERSATILE AND VERY NUTRITIOUS, PASTA IS AN ABSOLUTE MUST IN A HEALTHY, WELL-BALANCED DIET.

A complex carbohydrate food, pasta is made from wheat starch. In the case of the best Italian varieties, this means hard durum wheat, a wheat which is rich in protein, vitamins and minerals. Pasta combined with a small amount of another protein such as meat, pulses, eggs or cheese makes a complete protein meal, and this is the reason why pasta is traditionally served with these ingredients. It is well known that the Italians, like other people living around the Mediterranean, have long had one of the healthiest diets in the Western world, and nutritionists believe this is because of the combination of natural ingredients in their diet. Low-fat, high-fibre foods like pasta, bread, fresh fish, vegetables and fruit, plus olive oil and wine, feature high on their shopping lists, while processed foods and foods like butter and meat which are high in saturated animal fats are eaten in smaller quantities. The result is that the incidence of heart disease and other related problems is low in these countries, as it also is in the Orient, where pasta in the form of noodles and a diet low in animal fats combine together to keep heart disease at bay.

WHICH PASTA TO CHOOSE?

There are so many different shapes, sizes and colours of pasta available that it is often difficult to know which one to choose. Italian varieties are the most numerous, but oriental noodles must be included too.

Dried pasta

Dried pasta is very handy to keep in the storecupboard. It has a long shelf-life (it will keep up to 2 years), and it can be used at a moment's notice to make a quick and easy, nutritious meal.

There are literally hundreds of different types of pasta, so which do you choose? First and foremost, always check the label of Italian pasta before buying, to be sure that it is made from 'hard durum wheat semolina'; in Italian this is 'semola di grano duro'. If dried pasta is not made from this type of wheat, but from a cheaper, soft wheat, it will be less nutritious, difficult to cook and unpleasant to eat.

Pasta is also increasingly available in a wide choice of colours. Most pasta is pale yellow, made simply from flour and water. Darker yellow pasta indicates that eggs have been added – described as

'all'uovo' in Italian. This type contains more protein, and is usually more expensive. Green pasta, called 'pasta verde' in Italian, is flavoured with spinach; rose-coloured pasta, called 'pasta rosso', is flavoured with tomato. Two types of brown pasta are wholewheat and buckwheat. These are high in fibre and have a chewy texture. They take longer to cook than pasta made with white flour.

Many oriental noodles are made from wheat flour but tend to be paler in colour than the Italian varieties, unless they have eggs added, in which case they are yellow like Italian egg pasta. More interesting oriental noodles are often very thin and delicate in appearance and pure white in colour: these are made from rice flour or from a vegetable starch such as mung bean flour, and are often packed in bundles or skeins like wool. Sometimes they are pre-cooked and only need to be soaked in hot water before use, which makes them very quick and convenient to use.

Fresh pasta

There are far fewer varieties of fresh pasta available than of dried. They are interchangeable with the dried kinds and their nutritional value is the same. They are not quite so convenient, however, since they have a much shorter shelf-life – they will only keep for a few days in the chilling cabinet or refrigerator, or up to 3 months in the freezer. On the plus side, fresh pasta take far less time to cook than dried, and is much lighter in texture.

MAKING PASTA AT HOME

Fresh, homemade pasta is unbelievably light in texture, and it is very easy to make with only a few inexpensive ingredients.

Making pasta is similar to making bread and pastry, except that it is a little harder to roll out than pastry as the dough is elastic and must be very thin. An inexpensive pasta machine makes this job quicker and easier as it has special rollers which roll the dough quickly and evenly until it is paper thin, so that kneading is less important than when making it by hand.

Ingredients for making pasta

Commercially made pasta uses hard semolina flour. This is not easy to obtain, so the nearest equivalent is strong plain flour – the kind that is used for breadmaking. This flour has a high gluten content and therefore makes the dough easier to knead and roll out, which you will find especially helpful if you are kneading and rolling by hand. If you are making pasta with a machine, however, ordinary plain flour can be used.

Wholemeal flour can be substituted for white flour. It will give the pasta a nutty texture and flavour and increase its fibre content. If you find it too heavy, try combining half wholemeal with half white, which gives a lighter result.

Although pasta can be made simply with flour and water, most homemade recipes include eggs. Italian cooks prefer to use fresh eggs with deep yellow yolks to give the pasta a good colour.

Often a little olive oil is added to the dough, for added flavour and also to help with elasticity, particularly when making small pasta.

The same applies to the use of salt, which is traditionally included with the flour to help bring out the flavour of the pasta.

Flavoured pasta

If you are making pasta at home, the following 3 varieties are interesting to try.

Tomato Pasta: add 2-4 tablespoons tomato purée to the eggs before mixing in the flour.

Spinach Pasta: Add 75 g (3 oz) puréed spinach to the eggs before mixing in the flour.

Herb (and Garlic) Pasta: mix 2-4 tablespoons finely chopped fresh herbs with the flour. Crushed garlic can also be added to the eggs if you like, before mixing in the flour.

Rolling, cutting and shaping pasta

If you are using a pasta machine, once the dough is made it can be put through the rollers and cut immediately according to the manufacturer's instructions. If working by hand, the dough should be placed in a bowl, covered with a tea towel and left for about 20 minutes, to allow the gluten to relax.

Having made and 'relaxed' the dough, the next stage is to roll and cut it into shape. With a machine, the dough is put through the smooth rollers which miraculously roll it out to the required degree of thinness (there is a dial to regulate this), after which it is put through the 'cutting' roller to make long shapes such as lasagne or tagliatelle.

To roll out the dough by hand, put it on a lightly floured work surface and roll with a thin, straight rolling pin, reflouring the surface and rolling pin as necessary. Roll and stretch the dough as quickly as you can to prevent it drying out, turning the dough a quarter or half turn each time so that it stretches out evenly on all sides to make a paper-thin rectangle. If you are making shapes such as lasagne or tagliatelle, transfer the rectangle of dough to a lightly floured tea towel and leave it to rest for no longer than 1 hour. Cut the dough into rectangles or squares for lasagne; for tagliatelle roll it up like a Swiss roll and cut it into strips with a sharp knife. Place the shapes back on the tea towel and sprinkle them lightly with flour. They can be cooked immediately or kept for up to 24 hours. Leave them any longer and they will become dry and brittle. If you like, they can be frozen: leave them to dry out for 15 minutes, open freeze for about 1 hour, then pack in polythene bags and store in the freezer for up to 3 months. Pasta can then be cooked from frozen.

QUANTITIES OF PASTA

Pasta is usually eaten as a first course (*primo piatto*) in Italy, with a serving of 50-65 g (2-2½ oz) uncooked pasta per person, depending on the accompanying sauce. If you are serving pasta as a main course, increase this weight to 75-90 g (3-3½ oz) per person. The weight is the same whether the pasta is fresh or dried.

COOKING PASTA

Pasta is very simple to cook, but there are a few general rules to follow which will ensure that it does not overcook and stick together.

1. Use plenty of water – at least 750 ml (1¼ pints) water for every 125 g (4 oz) pasta – and the largest pan you have. Bring the water to the boil before adding the pasta. Salt is usually added – 1 teaspoon salt for every 2 litres (3½ pints) water should be sufficient. If you prefer not to use salt, lemon juice may be used instead. Sometimes a little oil is added to help prevent the pasta sticking together.

2. Once the water has come to the boil, tip in the pasta and stir it to separate the strands or shapes.

Turn up the heat and bring the water quickly back to the boil again, then reduce the heat so that the water is kept at a rolling boil. Time the cooking from this moment. Keep the pan uncovered, stirring the pasta occasionally.

3. Manufacturers generally give cooking times on packets of pasta, but times can vary according to the age of the pasta, the size of the pan, the quantity of water and the degree of heat. It is very easy to overcook pasta: the best way of judging whether it is ready or not is to taste it. The Italians say pasta is ready to eat when it is '*al dente*', which literally means 'to the tooth' or 'firm to the bite'. It should be tender, but with a slight resistance.

4. The moment it is ready, drain the pasta into a colander or large sieve and shake to remove as much water as possible. Remember that because the pasta is still cooking in its own heat it should be served immediately if it is not to overcook and become soggy. Serve according to the recipe. Always serve grated Parmesan cheese separately at the table rather than sprinkling it over the pasta or sauce before serving.

Cooking times

Check with manufacturer's instructions for precise timings, if available, but the following cooking times are a general guide for plain, unflavoured pasta:

Fresh pasta:
Unfilled: 2-3 minutes
Filled: 8-10 minutes

Dried pasta:
Unfilled: 8-12 minutes
Filled: about 15 minutes

BASIC EGG PASTA

300 g (10 oz) strong plain flour
½ teaspoon salt
3 eggs, beaten
1 tablespoon olive oil (optional)

Sift the flour and salt into a large bowl. Make a well in the centre and add the eggs and oil, if using. With a fork, gradually mix the flour into the eggs until the liquid has been absorbed. Continue mixing with your fingers, adding drops of water if necessary until the mixture comes together. If it becomes sticky, add a little flour. Knead the dough on the work surface for about 10 minutes until smooth and elastic, flouring your hands and the surface when necessary. To knead, fold the dough over towards you, then press it away from you with the heel of your hand. If you are not using a pasta machine, this is essential to make the dough elastic enough to be rolled out without difficulty.

MAKES A 300 G (10 OZ) QUANTITY

Nutritional content per quantity:	Carbohydrate: 240 g	Fat: 36 g	Fibre: 12 g	Kilocalories: 1400

Mixing the flour into the eggs

Mixing using the fingers

Kneading the dough

To make ravioli

After kneading and relaxing the dough, cut it in half and wrap one half in a damp tea towel. Roll the unwrapped half out to a paper-thin rectangle, reflouring the surface and rolling pin as necessary. Cover with a damp tea towel. Unwrap the other piece. Roll it out to the same size as the first.

Place small heaps of your chosen filling on the second rectangle of dough spacing them about 3.5 cm (1½ inches) apart. Brush water around each portion of filling and the 4 edges of the rectangle.

Uncover the first rectangle of dough and place it over the dough which has the filling on it. Press around the heaps of filling, then around the 4 edges. Press firmly, especially around the filling, so that a seal is made and all the air is pushed out.

Cut around each pile of filling with a serrated-edged pastry wheel, either in a round or square shape. Alternatively, you can use a plain or fluted pastry cutter. As each shape is cut, place it on a floured tea towel. Before boiling, leave the ravioli to dry out for 30 minutes, turning them over once.

Brushing water around each portion

Pressing down around the filling

Cutting out each ravioli

To make tortellini

After kneading and relaxing the dough, cut it into quarters and wrap 3 pieces in a damp tea towel. Roll out the unwrapped piece to a paper-thin rectangle, then cut it into long strips about 5.5cm (2¼ inches) wide. Using a plain or fluted pastry cutter, cut out 5 cm (2 inch) circles, re-rolling the trimmings to make as many circles as possible.

Put a pea-sized ball of filling in the centre of each circle. Brush all around the edge with water.

Fold the dough in half over the filling, so that the top and bottom edges do not quite meet. Press the edges together to seal them.

Pull the 2 corners of the semi-circle around your index finger to make 'navel' shapes. Press them together with a little water to seal them, then turn the outside, rounded edge upwards like the brim of a hat. As each shape is made, place it on a floured surface. Before boiling, leave the tortellini to dry for 30 minutes, turning them over once.

Pressing the edges together to seal them

Shaping the pasta round the index finger

Turning the outside edge upwards

ITALIAN PASTA SHAPES AND THEIR USES

PASTA	SHAPE	USE
Bucatini	Thick, tubular spaghetti	With thick and smooth sauces
Cannelloni	Large hollow tubes	For stuffing with meat, vegetables and fish; bake in a sauce or coat and deep-fry
Capelli d'angelo	'Angel's hair'; long, very thin vermicelli	With smooth sauces and in soups and desserts
Cappelletti	Small stuffed 'hats'	Stuffed with savoury fillings as for ravioli; served with melted butter or sauce
Chitarra	Square-shaped spaghetti	With most sauces, as for spaghetti
Conchiglie	Shells in many different sizes	With chunky and thick creamy sauces, and in salads
Farfalle	Bows or butterflies	With thin or thick sauces and in salads
Fedelini (also *spaghettini*)	Long, thin spaghetti	With smooth and creamy sauces
Fettuccine	Long, flat ribbon noodles from Rome; often sold coiled into nests, *a nidi*	With smooth and creamy sauces, in soufflés and desserts
Fusilli	Spirals, coils or springs; long or short	With thick or thin sauces and in salads
Lasagne	Flat rectangular or square sheets; sometimes ridged or with crinkled edges	For baking, in layers with meat, fish, vegetables and cheese sauce, or rolled around filling to make cannelloni
Linguine	Thin, flat ribbon noodle	As for fedelini and spaghetti
Lumache	Snails	As for conchiglie
Maccheroni	Thick, long and hollow, as short-cut 'elbow' macaroni	With thick and creamy sauces; good in baked dishes
Manicotte	Large tubes like cannelloni	For stuffing as for cannelloni
Marille	Short-cut 'designer' pasta; like several macaroni stuck together	As for short-cut maccheroni; particularly with thick or creamy sauces
Mezze Zite	Tubes, like thick maccheroni; *zita* are the same only larger	As for maccheroni
Paglia e Fieno	Flat ribbon noodles (spinach and egg pasta), coiled into nests	As for tagliatelle
Pastina	Tiny shapes (eg anellini, rings; conchigliette, shells; farfallette, bows or butterflies; orecchiette, ears; rotelline, rings; stelline, stars)	For soups and casseroles; good in children's dishes
Penne	Short, tubular 'quills' with angled ends; *penne rigate* are ridged	As for short-cut macaroni
Ravioli	Filled (round or square) small shapes, sometimes with serrated or fluted edges	With meat, poultry, fish, vegetable or cheese filling; served with melted butter or a sauce, or baked
Rigatoni	Short-cut, ridged tubes	As for short-cut macaroni
Rotelle (also *ruote*)	Cartwheels or wagon wheels	For children's meals and in soups, stews and salads
Spaghetti	Long, thin 'strings', spaghettini is thinner	For any kind of sauce, and in bakes and soufflés
Tagliatelle	Flat, ribbon noodle from northern Italy	Best with smooth sauces, thick or thin
Tortellini	Small stuffed 'navels'; tortelloni are the same shape only larger	Stuffed with savoury fillings as for ravioli; served with melted butter or sauce; can also be baked
Trenette	Narrow, flat ribbons	As for fedelini and spaghetti
Vermicelli	Thin pasta strands from Naples	As for spaghetti; and with Neapolitan sauces

Soups and starters

WHETHER FOR AN ELEGANT DINNER PARTY STARTER OR A HEARTY, WHOLESOME FAMILY SUPPER, THE VARIED SELECTION OF MOUTH WATERING ORIENTAL AND EUROPEAN RECIPES IN THIS FIRST CHAPTER CLEARLY ILLUSTRATE THE ENORMOUS VERSATILITY OF PASTA AS A BASIC INGREDIENT.

NOODLE SOUP

1 litre (1¾ pints) chicken stock or water
80 g (2.8 oz) packet dried instant noodles
  with wonton flavoured soup base
3 tablespoons medium dry sherry
1 tablespoon soy sauce
1 clove garlic, crushed
2.5 cm (1 inch) piece root ginger, chopped
200 g (7 oz) fresh spinach, stalks removed,
  washed and torn into shreds
300 g (10 oz) silken tofu (bean curd), drained
  and cut into strips
2-3 teaspoons sesame seeds, according to taste
salt and pepper

Pour the stock or water into a large saucepan. Add the soup base, sherry, soy sauce, garlic and ginger and bring to the boil.

Add the noodles and spinach and simmer for 3 minutes. Add the tofu and simmer for a further 1-2 minutes until it is heated through. Adjust the seasoning, if necessary, and sprinkle with the sesame seeds before serving. Serve with sesame seed bread or rolls.

SERVES 4

Nutritional content per serving: Carbohydrate: 24 g   Fat: 5 g   Fibre: 1 g   Kilocalories: 190

VEGETABLE MINESTRONE WITH PESTO SAUCE

2 tablespoons olive oil
1 small onion, chopped finely
1 small courgette, diced finely
2 celery sticks, chopped finely
2 carrots, sliced thinly
1 potato, diced
1 small aubergine, diced finely
50 g (2 oz) green beans, cut into 2-3 pieces
50 g (2 oz) tiny cauliflower florets
50 g (2 oz) fresh spinach, shredded
1.2 litres (2 pints) vegetable stock or water
125 g (4 oz) dried medium pasta shapes
  (bows or shells)
1 × 220 g (8 oz) can borlotti or butter
  beans, drained and rinsed
salt and pepper
SAUCE:
1 clove garlic
1 tablespoon pine kernels
2 tablespoons chopped basil
2 tablespoons olive oil
TO GARNISH:
chopped parsley
grated Cheddar cheese

Heat the oil in a heavy pan. Add the onion and stir over a gentle heat until it is golden. Add the vegetables and cook for 5-10 minutes, stirring gently. Pour in the stock or water and bring to the boil. Season and reduce the heat, cover and simmer for 15 minutes.

Add the pasta shapes and cook, covered, for a further 10-12 minutes, or according to the instructions given on the packet.

Meanwhile, make the pesto sauce. Pound the garlic, pine kernels and basil in a mortar and pestle and gradually work in the oil.

Add the borlotti or butter beans to the soup, stir and cook for a further 3-5 minutes or until they are heated through and the pasta is cooked. Adjust the seasoning if necessary and transfer the soup to a heated serving bowl. At the moment of serving, stir the pesto sauce into the soup. Garnish with chopped parsley and grated Cheddar. Serve with breadsticks or crusty bread.

Microwave: Place the oil in a bowl and cook on High Power for 1 minute. Add the onion, cover and cook on High Power for 2 minutes. Add the vegetables, re-cover and cook on High Power for 8 minutes, stirring once. Add the hot stock, cover and cook on High Power for 10 minutes. Add the pasta, cover and cook on High Power for a further 10 minutes. Meanwhile prepare the sauce as above. Add the beans to the soup and cook on High Power for 2 minutes. Serve as above.

SERVES 4-6

Nutritional content per serving: Carbohydrate: 65 g   Fat: 18 g   Fibre: 16 g   Kilocalories: 480

Noodle Soup; Vegetable Minestrone with Pesto Sauce

PRAWN RAVIOLI IN FISH BROTH

LARGE FRESH MEDITERRANEAN PRAWNS ARE BEST FOR THIS ORIENTAL-INSPIRED DISH, WHICH IS A CROSS BETWEEN A SOUP AND A STARTER. SMALL FROZEN PEELED PRAWNS CAN BE USED, BUT YOU WILL NEED TO PUT SEVERAL TOGETHER IN EACH RAVIOLI. MAKE SURE THEY ARE DEFROSTED AND THOROUGHLY DRIED BEFORE USE. FISH STOCK CUBES CAN BE USED FOR THE BROTH, BUT YOU WILL GET A MORE AUTHENTIC FLAVOUR IF YOU MAKE YOUR OWN STOCK WITH SOME FISH BONES AND HEADS AND THE SHELLS FROM THE PRAWNS

12 Mediterranean prawns, shells removed and
　halved
2 tablespoons finely chopped coriander
2 sticks lemon grass or finely pared rind of
　2 limes or 1 large lemon
1 litre (1¾ pints) fish stock
salt and pepper
RAVIOLI DOUGH:
125 g (4 oz) strong plain flour
salt
1 egg, beaten
1 tablespoon olive oil
TO GARNISH:
parsley sprigs
pared lime rind (optional)

First make the ravioli dough. Sift the flour and 2 pinches of salt into a bowl. Mix in the egg, then the oil. Turn the dough out on to a floured surface and knead with floured hands until it is shiny and smooth – about 10 minutes. Cut the dough in half and wrap one half in a damp tea towel. Roll the other half out to a paper-thin rectangle, 36 × 24 cm (14½ × 9½ inches), reflouring the surface and the rolling pin as necessary. Cover with a damp tea towel.

Unwrap the other piece of dough and roll it out to a rectangle the same size as the first. Place the prawn halves on this piece of dough at regular intervals, 4 prawn halves across the width of the dough and 6 along the length. Sprinkle each prawn half with a little of the chopped coriander and salt and pepper to taste.

Brush water around the edges of the dough and all around each prawn half, then place the first piece of dough on top. Press it down firmly, especially around each prawn half, to make a good seal and exclude any air from the separate parcels of dough.

Cut around each prawn half with a serrated-edged ravioli wheel, either in round or square shapes. As each one is cut, place it on a floured baking sheet. Leave the ravioli to dry for 1-2 hours.

If using lemon grass, bruise it by pounding it with a pestle. Pour the fish stock into a large saucepan. Bring it to the boil, add the lemon grass, if used, or the lime or lemon rind, and the remaining coriander. Add the ravioli, stir well and bring back to the boil. Reduce the heat and boil for 5 minutes or until the pasta is *al dente*, stirring frequently so that the ravioli cook evenly. Taste the stock and adjust the seasoning if necessary before serving. Garnish with parsley and lime rind, if desired. No accompaniment is necessary.

Microwave: Prepare the ravioli dough as above then make the prawn stuffed ravioli. Place the fish stock in a large bowl, cover and cook on High Power for 6-8 minutes or until boiling. Add the lemon grass, or the lime or lemon rind and remaining coriander. Add the ravioli and cook for 4 minutes or until *al dente*. Leave to stand for 2 minutes. Adjust the seasoning if necessary and serve as above.

SERVES 4

Nutritional content per serving:	Carbohydrate: 25 g	Fat: 7 g	Fibre: 1 g	Kilocalories: 230

Prawn Ravioli in Fish Broth; Pasta in Broth

PASTA IN BROTH

250 g (8 oz) chicken pieces, chopped
    (including any bones and skin)
250 g (8 oz) boneless stewing beef, cubed
1 carrot, chopped roughly
1 celery stick, chopped
1 large onion
4-6 cloves
1 clove garlic, halved
4-6 black peppercorns
1 bouquet garni
200 g (7 oz) dried tiny soup pasta
salt and pepper
TO GARNISH:
celery leaves
marjoram sprigs

Put the chicken and beef in a large saucepan. Pour in 1.2 litres (2 pints) of cold water and bring it to the boil. Skim off any scum that rises to the surface.

Add the carrot and celery, the onion studded with the cloves, the garlic, peppercorns and bouquet garni. Season to taste. Bring back to the boil. Reduce the heat, half cover the saucepan and simmer very gently for 1-2 hours according to the time available. (The longer the stock is left to cook the more flavoursome the broth will be.) Top up with more cold water from time to time if necessary.

Strain the stock through a fine sieve into a clean saucepan. Skim off any fat. Bring the stock to the boil and add the pasta. Cover the pan and boil for 10 minutes, or according to the instructions for boiling pasta given on the packet. Adjust the seasoning if necessary. Garnish with celery leaves and marjoram sprigs and serve hot.

Freezing: is recommended. Freeze without the pasta in an airtight rigid container. This will keep for up to 3 months. Defrost in a refrigerator overnight or at room temperature for 4-6 hours, then reheat until bubbling. Add the pasta and complete the recipe.

SERVES 4

Nutritional content per serving: Carbohydrate: 42 g   Fibre: 2 g   Kilocalories: 190

ITALIAN PASTA AND BEAN SOUP

125 g (4 oz) pinto beans, soaked overnight
125 g (4 oz) haricot beans, soaked overnight
175 g (6 oz) smoked bacon, derinded and
chopped or lean salt pork, derinded and
diced
1 onion, chopped finely
1 carrot, chopped finely
1 celery stick, chopped finely
2 cloves garlic, crushed
1.4 litres (2½ pints) beef stock
1 small ham bone (knuckle)
250 g (8 oz) dried tagliatelle, broken into
4-5 cm (1½-2 inch) pieces
2 tablespoons finely chopped parsley
salt and pepper

Put the bacon or pork in a heavy pan and place it over moderate heat until the fat runs. Increase the heat and continue cooking, stirring occasionally, until the bacon or pork is crisp. Remove and set aside.

Add the onion, carrot and celery to the pan. Cook for 10-15 minutes, stirring, until soft. Drain the beans and add to the pan with the garlic, bacon or pork and three quarters of the stock. Boil and add the bone, cover and simmer for 1½-2 hours until the beans are soft.

Remove the bone and cut the meat from it into cubes, discarding the skin and fat. Put the meat back into the soup and add the remaining stock. Bring to the boil. Add the pasta, half the parsley and season to taste. Cook for 10-15 minutes, stirring. Sprinkle with parsley.

Microwave: Soak the beans. Place the bacon in a bowl and cook on High Power for 6 minutes. Remove with a slotted spoon, add the onion, carrot and celery, cover and cook on High Power for 6 minutes. Add the drained beans, garlic, bacon, 1.2 litres (2 pints) of the boiling stock and ham bone. Cook covered on High Power for 10 minutes. Reduce power and cook on Medium Power for 40 minutes. Remove the meat from the bone as above. Add the remaining stock, pasta, half the parsley and seasoning. Cover and cook on High Power for 8 minutes, stirring once. Leave covered, for 5 minutes before serving.

SERVES 4-6

Nutritional content per serving: Carbohydrate: 85 g   Fat: 6 g   Fibre: 20 g   Kilocalories: 535

Italian Pasta and Bean Soup

Laksa

LAKSA

THIS SPICY, COCONUT MILK SOUP COMES FROM SINGAPORE, WHERE THE INGREDIENTS VARY ACCORDING TO WHAT IS IN SEASON

3 tablespoons groundnut or corn oil

4 spring onions, chopped finely

2.5 cm (1 inch) piece root ginger, chopped finely

1-2 cloves garlic, crushed

1 tablespoon mild curry powder

1 teaspoon ground turmeric

125 g (4 oz) pork fillet, cut into thin strips

1.4 litres (2½ pints) chicken stock

125 g (4 oz) creamed coconut, dissolved in 300 ml (½ pint) water

2 tablespoons soy sauce

2 carrots, cut into julienne strips

125 g (4 oz) green beans, topped, tailed and cut in half diagonally

125 g (4 oz) peeled prawns

125 g (4 oz) fresh bean sprouts

125 g (4 oz) dried Chinese egg noodles

salt and pepper

unpeeled prawns to garnish

Heat the oil in a large, heavy saucepan. Add the spring onions, ginger and garlic and cook gently, stirring, until the ingredients give off a spicy aroma. Stir in the curry powder and turmeric, then the pork fillet. Cook gently for 5 minutes, stirring all the time. Pour in the stock, coconut 'milk' and soy sauce and bring to the boil. Cover and simmer gently for 10 minutes, stirring occasionally.

Add the carrots and green beans and simmer, uncovered, for 5 minutes. Add the prawns and bean sprouts and simmer for a further 2-3 minutes.

Cut the noodles into short lengths with scissors. Add them to the soup and bring the liquid back to the boil. Cover the pan tightly and remove it from the heat. Leave it to stand for 5 minutes, or until the noodles are *al dente*. Taste and add seasoning, if necessary, before serving. Garnish with unpeeled prawns, and serve with deep-fried prawn crackers.

SERVES 4-6

Nutritional content per serving: Carbohydrate: 30 g   Fat: 28 g   Fibre: 4 g   Kilocalories: 450

CURRIED FISH AND NOODLE SOUP

THIS BURMESE SPECIALITY, KNOWN AS *MOHINGHA*, IS REAL ORIENTAL 'FAST FOOD'. IT IS SOLD ON STREET CORNERS IN VIRTUALLY EVERY TOWN IN BURMA – PASSERS-BY STOP AND EAT IT STANDING UP!

175 g (6 oz) desiccated coconut
750-900 g (1½-2 lb) fresh mackerel, filleted
1-2 stems lemon grass, chopped roughly, or
  2-3 strips of lime or lemon rind
4 onions, chopped roughly
4-6 cloves garlic, chopped roughly
2.5 cm (1 inch) piece fresh root ginger,
  peeled and chopped roughly
2-3 green chillies, deseeded and sliced thinly,
  or ½ teaspoon chilli powder
1 teaspoon ground turmeric
1 tablespoon fish sauce or vinegar, or
  according to taste
6 tablespoons groundnut oil
2 tablespoons cornflour
250 g (8 oz) thread egg noodles
lime or lemon juice, to taste
salt and pepper
spring onions, chopped finely to garnish

First make the coconut 'milk'. Place the desiccated coconut in a bowl, pour over 1.2 litres (2 pints) boiling water and stir. Cover the bowl tightly and leave to stand.

Meanwhile, put the mackerel fillets in a large flameproof casserole. Pour in 300 ml (½ pint) cold water and bring to the boil. Cover and simmer for 5 minutes. Lift out the fish, pour the cooking liquid into a bowl and rinse the casserole.

Place the lemon grass or lime or lemon rind in a food processor with the onions, garlic, ginger, chillies, turmeric and fish sauce or vinegar to taste. Blend to a purée. Heat the oil in the casserole and add the purée. Cover and cook gently for about 15 minutes, or until the pieces of onion are tender. Uncover and cook for a further 15 minutes, stirring frequently, until golden brown.

Add the reserved cooking liquid to the casserole and strain in the coconut 'milk'. Bring the liquid to the boil, stirring. Mix the cornflour to a paste with 4 tablespoons cold water, add it to the pan and simmer for about 5 minutes, stirring, until the liquid has thickened.

Meanwhile, bring a saucepan of salted water to the boil. Add the noodles, cover tightly and remove it from the heat. Leave it to stand, covered, for 6 minutes or according to packet instructions.

Cut the mackerel into chunks and add to the soup with lime or lemon juice and salt and pepper to taste. Heat through gently. Drain the noodles and divide equally between 4 warm soup bowls. Ladle the soup on top and garnish with finely chopped spring onions to serve.

Microwave: Prepare the coconut milk as above. Place the fish in a shallow dish with ½ pint (300 ml) hot water, cover and cook on High Power for 5 minutes, rearranging once. Remove the fish and reserve the liquor. Prepare the onion paste as above. Place the oil in a casserole and cook on High Power for 3 minutes. Add the paste and cook on High Power, uncovered, for 10 minutes, stirring once. Add the reserved liquor and strained coconut milk. Cook on High Power for 5 minutes, or until boiling. Add the dissolved cornflour and cook on High Power for 3 minutes, stirring once. Place the noodles in a bowl with 1.2 litres (2 pints) boiling water. Cook on High Power for 6 minutes then drain. Add to the soup with the fish, lemon juice and salt and pepper. Reheat on High Power for 2-3 minutes until hot. Serve as above.

SERVES 6-8

Nutritional content per serving: Carbohydrate: 38 g   Fat: 32 g   Fibre: 4 g   Kilocalories: 520

Curried Fish and Noodle Soup; Chinese Shredded Pork and Noodle Soup

CHINESE SHREDDED PORK AND NOODLE SOUP

THE FLAVOUR OF THE CHICKEN STOCK IS QUITE IMPORTANT IN THIS SOUP, SO TRY TO MAKE YOUR OWN IF POSSIBLE

1.2 litres (2 pints) chicken stock
2 tablespoons soy sauce
1 tablespoon vinegar
1 tablespoon medium dry sherry
250 g (8 oz) pork fillet, cut diagonally into
　3.5 × 1 cm (1½ × ½ inch) strips
3 spring onions, sliced diagonally
2.5 cm (1 inch) piece fresh root ginger, peeled
　and cut into very fine julienne
125 g (4 oz) button mushrooms, sliced thinly
200 g (7 oz) Chinese leaves, shredded
125 g (4 oz) bean sprouts
125 g (4 oz) medium egg noodles
salt and pepper

Place the stock in a large saucepan and bring it to the boil. Add the soy sauce, vinegar, sherry, pork strips, spring onions, ginger and mushrooms. Stir once, cover the pan and simmer for 10 minutes, stirring occasionally.

　　Add the Chinese leaves and cook for a further 5 minutes. Add the bean sprouts and noodles and season with salt and pepper to taste. Cook for 5 minutes more, or until the noodles are tender. Adjust the seasoning if necessary before serving. Serve extra soy sauce separately, for those who like its pronounced flavour.

SERVES 4

Nutritional content per serving:　Carbohydrate: 27 g　Fat: 7 g　Fibre 3 g　Kilocalories: 275

Catalan pasta, meat and vegetable soup

Serve the broth and pasta as a first course 'soup', followed by the meat and vegetables as a main course

2 tablespoons olive oil
4 rashers unsmoked streaky bacon, derinded
  and chopped finely
2 celery sticks, sliced thinly
2 chicken portions
500 g (1 lb) shin of veal, with bone (*osso buco*)
1 small ham bone (knuckle)
3 cloves garlic, chopped finely
½ teaspoon ground cinnamon
250 g (8 oz) black pudding, sliced thickly
2 carrots, sliced lengthways
2 leeks, trimmed and chopped roughly
3 small (young) turnips, quartered
375 g (12 oz) small new potatoes, halved or
  quartered
1 × 432 g (15.2 oz) can chick peas, drained
125 g (4 oz) dried pasta shells
salt and pepper
TO SERVE:
1-2 tablespoons olive oil, to taste
chopped parsley

Heat the oil in a large, heavy saucepan or flameproof casserole. Add the bacon and celery and cook gently, stirring frequently, until they are lightly coloured – about 5 minutes. Add the chicken, veal and ham bone and cover generously with water. Add the garlic and cinnamon and season with salt and pepper to taste. (Take care when adding salt as the ham may be salty.) Bring to the boil and remove any scum that rises to the surface with a slotted spoon. Cover the pan and simmer for 1¼ hours, skimming occasionally and adding water if necessary.

Add the black pudding, carrots, leeks, turnips and potatoes. Cover and continue cooking for a further 30 minutes or until the vegetables are tender and the meat is literally falling from the bones. Add the chick peas for the last 10 minutes or so, to heat them through.

Strain the cooking liquid through a fine sieve into a pan. Skim off any fat with a slotted spoon. Bring to the boil and add the pasta. Stir and boil for 10 minutes, or according to packet instructions.

Meanwhile, cut the meats into serving pieces, discarding the skin, fat and bones. Arrange them on a warm serving platter with the vegetables. Cover the platter loosely and set it aside to keep warm.

Taste the broth and pasta and adjust the seasoning if necessary. Ladle the broth into warm soup plates as a first course, garnished with parsley sprigs. Sprinkle the olive oil and parsley over the meats and vegetables and serve them separately as a main course.

Microwave: Place the oil in a bowl and cook on High Power for 1 minute. Add the bacon and celery and cook on High Power for 5 minutes, stirring once. Add the chicken, veal and ham bone and cover with boiling water. Add the garlic, cinnamon and seasoning. Cover and cook on High Power for 10 minutes. Skim well, reduce the power to Medium Power, re-cover and cook for a further 40-50 minutes, stirring and skimming to remove scum twice. Add the black pudding and remaining vegetables. Cover and cook on High Power for 20-25 minutes, stirring twice (add a little more boiling water during cooking if necessary) and adding the chick peas for the last 5 minutes cooking time. Strain the cooking liquid and skim off any fat. Return to another bowl and cook on High Power for 3-5 minutes or until boiling. Add the pasta and cook on High Power for 10 minutes, stirring once. Cover and leave to stand for 3 minutes. Meanwhile remove the meat from the chicken, veal and ham bones. Cut into serving pieces then mix with the vegetables. Serve as above.

SERVES 4-6

Nutritional content per serving of soup only: Carbohydrate: 26 g   Fibre: 1 g   Kilocalories: 120

Catalan Pasta, Meat and Vegetable Soup; Sicilian Fish Soup

SICILIAN FISH SOUP

4 tablespoons olive oil

1 onion, sliced thinly

2 celery sticks, sliced

4 cloves garlic, crushed

1 large pinch of saffron threads or 1 sachet powdered saffron

375 g (12 oz) ripe tomatoes, skinned and chopped roughly

3 tablespoons chopped parsley

2 bay leaves

1.2 litres (2 pints) fish stock or water

150 ml (¼ pint) dry white wine

125 g (4 oz) small pasta shapes (spirals, bows, etc)

900 g (2 lb) mixed white fish (monkfish, halibut, cod, mullet, haddock), skinned, boned and cut into bite-sized pieces

salt and pepper

unshelled prawns to garnish

Heat the oil in a large, heavy saucepan. Add the onion and celery and stir gently over a low heat until they have softened. Stir in the garlic, saffron, tomatoes, 2 tablespoons of the parsley and the bay leaves and season with salt and pepper to taste. Cook gently, stirring to break up the tomatoes, for 5 minutes.

Pour in the stock or water and the wine and bring to the boil. Cover and simmer for 15 minutes, stirring occasionally.

Add the pasta and bring the liquid back to the boil. Let it boil, uncovered, for 5 minutes. Reduce the heat and add the fish with the firmest flesh and cook for about 10 minutes. Add the fish with the thinner, more delicate flesh and simmer for a further 5 minutes or until all of the fish and the pasta are cooked. Adjust the seasoning if necessary. Serve garnished with the remaining parsley and the prawns. Serve with toasted slices of French bread.

SERVES 4-6

Nutritional content per serving: Carbohydrate: 32 g   Fat: 18 g   Fibre: 3 g   Kilocalories: 485

MEATY MILANESE MINESTRONE

2 tablespoons olive oil

2 rashers smoked streaky bacon, derinded and chopped finely

1 onion, chopped finely

2 carrots, diced finely

2 celery sticks, chopped finely

2 cloves garlic, crushed

1.4 litres (2½ pints) chicken stock

2 potatoes, peeled and diced

4 ripe tomatoes, skinned and chopped roughly

2 teaspoons tomato purée

1 teaspoon dried mixed herbs

1 teaspoon dried marjoram or basil

75 g (3 oz) frozen petits pois

75 g (3 oz) dried macaroni

175 g (6 oz) cooked chicken

75 g (3 oz) salami in one piece, skinned and cut into chunks

salt and pepper

marjoram sprigs to garnish

Heat the oil in a heavy pan. Add the bacon, onion, carrots and celery and cook, stirring, until they are soft. Add the garlic. Pour in the stock and bring to the boil. Add the potatoes, tomatoes, purée and herbs and seasoning. Cover and simmer for 20 minutes.

Add the petits pois and cook for 5 minutes more. Add the pasta, cover again and cook for a further 10-12 minutes, or according to the instructions for boiling pasta given on the packet. About 5 minutes before the pasta is ready, bone, skin and chop the chicken into bite size pieces. Add the chicken and salami to the soup and heat them through. Garnish with marjoram sprigs. Serve hot, with crusty bread.

Microwave: Place the oil in a bowl and cook on High Power for 1 minute. Add the bacon, onion, carrots and celery. Cover and cook on High Power for 8 minutes, stirring once. Add the garlic and hot stock, cover and cook on High Power for 5 minutes. Add the potatoes, tomatoes, purée and herbs, and season. Re-cover and cook on High Power for 10 minutes. Add the pasta, cover and cook on High Power for 10 minutes, stirring once. Add the chicken and salami and cook on High Power for 2 minutes. Serve as above.

SERVES 4-6

Nutritional content per serving: Carbohydrate: 35 g   Fat: 21 g   Fibre: 6 g   Kilocalories: 410

VERMICELLI WITH NEAPOLITAN TOMATO SAUCE

4 tablespoons olive oil

2 cloves garlic, crushed

750 g (1½ lb) ripe tomatoes, skinned and chopped coarsely

1 sprig basil

½ teaspoon ground cinnamon

250-300 g (8-10 oz) dried vermicelli

salt and pepper

Heat the oil in a heavy pan, add the garlic and fry gently until it begins to change colour. Add the tomatoes, basil, cinnamon and seasoning. Cover and simmer for 15 minutes, stirring frequently.

Meanwhile, bring a pan of salted water to the boil. Add the pasta, stir and bring back to the boil. Reduce the heat and boil, uncovered, for 10 minutes, or according to packet instructions. Drain the pasta and divide between 4 warm plates. Pour the sauce over and serve.

Freezing: is recommended for the sauce. Freeze in an airtight container. This will keep for up to 2 months. Defrost at room temperature for 2-3 hours, then reheat and continue as above.

SERVES 4

Nutritional content per serving: Carbohydrate: 51 g   Fat: 20 g   Fibre: 6 g   Kilocalories: 405

Meaty Milanese Minestrone; Vermicelli with Neapolitan Tomato Sauce

RIGATONI WITH SHELLFISH IN SAFFRON SAUCE

1 kg (2 lb) fresh mussels, soaked in cold water
  for 1 hour
250 g (8 oz) unshelled prawns
6 shelled scallops
2 tablespoons olive oil
1 small onion, chopped roughly
2 cloves garlic, chopped roughly
2 dried red chillies, chopped roughly
250 ml (8 fl oz) dry white wine
1-2 parsley sprigs
15 g (½ oz) butter
1 tablespoon plain flour
200 ml (7 fl oz) double cream
½ teaspoon powdered saffron
250-300 g (8-10 oz) dried rigatoni or
  macaroni
salt and pepper
parsley sprigs to garnish

Drain the mussels. Discard any open ones that do not close when tapped sharply on the work surface. Scrub the closed mussels under cold running water and remove the beards. Shell the prawns, reserving a whole one for garnish. Finely slice the scallops, including the coral.

Heat the oil in a large, heavy saucepan. Add the onion, garlic and chillies and cook gently, stirring frequently, until they have just softened – about 5 minutes. Pour in the wine and add the parsley sprigs. Bring to the boil. Add the mussels, cover the pan tightly and cook over a high heat for 6-8 minutes. Shake the pan vigorously from time to time, until all the mussels have opened.

Remove the mussels from the pan and strain the cooking liquid into a jug. When the mussels are cool enough to handle, remove the meat from the shells, holding the mussels over the jug to catch the juice. Discard any mussels that have not opened.

Melt the butter in the pan in which the mussels were cooked. Add the scallops and cook them gently for 5 minutes. Remove with a slotted spoon and set them aside with the mussels.

Mix the flour with a little of the cream to make a paste and add it to the pan. Stir over a gentle heat for 1-2 minutes. Gradually stir in the strained cooking liquid. Add the saffron and bring the liquid to the boil. Reduce until thickened to a coating consistency, stirring all the time.

Remove the pan from the heat, add the remaining cream and season with salt and pepper to taste. Return the mussels and scallops to the pan, add the shelled prawns and stir very gently to combine them with the sauce.

Bring a large saucepan of salted water to the boil. Add the rigatoni, stir and bring back to the boil. Reduce the heat slightly and boil, uncovered, for 10 minutes, or according to the packet instructions, stirring occasionally.

Just before the rigatoni is ready, reheat the sauce gently and adjust the seasoning if necessary. Drain the rigatoni well and turn it into a warm serving bowl. Pour over the sauce and toss quickly to coat the pasta. Serve at once, garnished with the reserved prawns and sprigs of parsley. Serve with the same wine that was used for cooking.

SERVES 4

Nutritional content per serving: Carbohydrate: 59 g   Fat: 30 g   Fibre: 2 g   Kilocalories: 640

Rigatoni with Shellfish in Saffron Sauce; Tagliatelle with Radicchio and Cream

TAGLIATELLE WITH RADICCHIO AND CREAM

HAVE THE PAN OF BOILING SALTED WATER READY FOR THE PASTA BEFORE YOU START MAKING THE SAUCE, PLUS A LARGE, WARM SERVING BOWL, AS THE SAUCE IS BEST SERVED VERY FRESH

250 g (8 oz) radicchio
50 g (2 oz) butter
1 tablespoon olive oil
1 onion, chopped very finely
150 ml (¼ pint) double cream
250-300 g (8-10 oz) fresh tagliatelle
50 g (2 oz) freshly grated Parmesan cheese
salt and pepper

Shred the radicchio finely, reserving a few small, curly inner leaves for the garnish. Melt the butter with the oil in a large, heavy saucepan. Add the onion and cook gently, stirring frequently, until it is softened – about 10 minutes.

Add the shredded radicchio and cook, stirring, over a moderate heat, until it wilts and begins to turn brown. Add salt to taste and plenty of pepper. Stir in the cream and heat it through.

Plunge the pasta into a pan of boiling salted water, stir and bring back to the boil. Reduce the heat and boil, uncovered, for 3-4 minutes, or according to the packet instructions, stirring occasionally.

Drain the tagliatelle well. Taste the sauce and adjust the seasoning if necessary. Place the tagliatelle in a warm serving bowl, pour over the sauce and add the grated Parmesan cheese. Toss quickly to combine. Serve at once, garnished with the reserved radicchio leaves. Serve with a dry Italian white wine.

SERVES 4

Nutritional content per serving: Carbohydrate: 30 g   Fat: 33 g   Fibre: 3 g   Kilocalories: 430

PASTA WITH PEAS

250 g (8 oz) dried penne (quills) or short-cut macaroni
2 tablespoons olive oil
125 g (4 oz) frozen petits pois
25 g (1 oz) butter
1 onion, chopped finely
2 cloves garlic, crushed
175 g (6 oz) lean boiled ham, trimmed of all fat and cut into 1 cm (½ inch) squares
1 tablespoon chopped parsley
5-6 tablespoons chicken stock
2-3 tablespoons freshly grated Parmesan cheese
salt and pepper

Bring a large saucepan of salted water to the boil. Add the pasta and half of the oil and bring back to the boil. Stir, reduce the heat slightly and boil, uncovered, according to packet instructions – 8-10 minutes.

Meanwhile, cook the peas in boiling salted water for 5 minutes and drain well. Heat the remaining oil with the butter in a heavy, flameproof casserole. Add the onion and cook it gently until golden. Add the peas and garlic and cook for 1-2 minutes, stirring well. Add the ham and parsley and season to taste. Add the stock 1 tablespoon at a time and cook, stirring, until the sauce is well heated through.

Drain the pasta well and turn it into a warm serving bowl. Pour over the sauce and toss it well to combine it with the pasta. Add 2-3 tablespoons grated Parmesan cheese and toss again. Serve at once.

Microwave: Place the pasta in a bowl with 1.2 litres (2 pints) boiling salted water and half of the oil and cook on High Power for 10 minutes, stirring once. Cover and leave to stand for 3 minutes before draining. Place the peas in a bowl with 2 teaspoons water, cover and cook on High Power for 3 minutes, stirring once. Place the remaining oil and butter in a bowl and cook on High Power for 1-1½ minutes to melt. Add the onion and cook on High Power for 3 minutes. Add the peas and garlic and cook on High Power for 1 minute. Add the ham and parsley, and season. Add the stock and cook on High Power for 1 minute. Drain the pasta and serve as above.

SERVES 4

Nutritional content per serving: Carbohydrate: 56 g   Fat: 33 g   Fibre: 6 g   Kilocalories: 470

TAGLIATELLE WITH DOLCELATTE CHEESE SAUCE

25 g (1 oz) butter
175 g (6 oz) Dolcelatte cheese, rind removed, diced
150 ml (¼ pint) double cream
2 teaspoons finely chopped sage
250-300 g (8-10 oz) fresh tagliatelle
salt and pepper
sage sprigs to garnish

Melt the butter in a heavy saucepan. Add the cheese and place the pan over a very low heat until the cheese has melted. Gradually stir in the cream, beating vigorously with a wooden spoon so that it blends into the cheese. Remove the pan from the heat, stir in the sage and cover.

Bring a large saucepan of salted water to the boil. Add the tagliatelle, stir and bring back to the boil. Reduce the heat slightly and boil, uncovered, according to the packet instructions – 3-4 minutes.

Just before the pasta is ready, reheat the sauce and add pepper.

Drain the tagliatelle well and divide it equally between 4 warm soup plates. Pour the sauce over the pasta and garnish with sage.

SERVES 4

Nutritional content per serving: Carbohydrate: 17 g   Fat: 33 g   Fibre: 1 g   Kilocalories: 420

Pasta with Peas; Tagliatelle with Dolcelatte Cheese Sauce; Spaghetti with Olive Oil and Garlic

SPAGHETTI WITH OLIVE OIL AND GARLIC

250-300 g (8-10 oz) fresh or dried spaghetti
5 tablespoons extra-virgin Italian olive oil
4 cloves garlic, chopped finely or crushed
1-2 dried red chillies, chopped finely
  (optional)
salt and pepper

Bring a large saucepan of salted water to the boil. Add the spaghetti, stir and bring back to the boil. Reduce the heat slightly and boil uncovered, for 3-4 minutes for fresh pasta, 10-12 minutes for dried, or according to the instructions on the packet. When the spaghetti is cooked pour it into a colander and drain it well.

Heat the oil in the saucepan and add the garlic and chillies, if using. Cook over a moderate heat stirring constantly until it is sizzling. Tip in the spaghetti and toss vigorously to coat each strand in the flavoured oil. Serve at once, sprinkled with pepper. Serve with Italian or French bread and a fruity red or white wine.

SERVES 4

Nutritional content per serving: Carbohydrate: 54 g   Fat: 19 g   Fibre: 2 g   Kilocalories: 410

CRESPELLE

THESE ARE A KIND OF FILLED PANCAKE OR TURNOVER MADE FROM PASTA DOUGH. THEY ARE OFTEN TO BE FOUND ON THE MENUS OF ITALIAN RESTAURANTS, SOMETIMES CALLED *CRESPELLINI*, WHICH ARE THE SMALLER VERSION

75 g (3 oz) Mortadella, derinded
75 g (3 oz) cooked ham
125 g (4 oz) Mozzarella cheese, diced
1 tablespoon finely chopped oregano or basil
pepper
DOUGH:
125 g (4 oz) strong plain flour
salt
1 egg, beaten
1 tablespoon olive oil
SAUCE:
1 × 397 g (14 oz) can tomatoes
2 tablespoons olive oil
1 clove garlic
1 teaspoon finely chopped oregano or basil
1 teaspoon finely chopped parsley
salt and pepper

Cut the Mortadella and ham into 1 cm (½ inch) wide strips, and cut the strips across to make 1 cm (½ inch) squares. Place them in a bowl and stir in the diced Mozzarella, the oregano or basil, and pepper to taste, mixing well.

To make the dough, sift the flour and 2 pinches of salt into a bowl. Mix in the egg and add the oil. Turn the dough out on to a floured surface and knead with floured hands until it is shiny and smooth – about 10 minutes. Roll out the dough and cut it into eight 15 cm (6 inch) squares. Put one eighth of the filling mixture on one half of each square, arranging it on the diagonal to form a triangular shape. Brush the edges of the pasta with water, then fold over the unfilled side of the square to form a triangular parcel. Press the cut edges to seal them and fold them over by about 1 cm (½ inch) and mark them with the prongs of a fork. Leave to rest on a floured surface while making the sauce.

Put the tomatoes and their juice in a bowl and mash with a fork. Heat the oil in a heavy saucepan. Add the garlic and fry gently until it is golden brown. Remove the garlic from the oil with a slotted spoon and discard it. Add the tomatoes to the oil. Bring to the boil and cook over a moderate heat for 20 minutes, stirring occasionally. Reduce the heat, add the herbs and season with salt and pepper to taste. Cook for a further 5 minutes. Remove from the heat.

Pour half the tomato sauce into a large baking dish. Arrange the crespelle on top in a single layer. Do not overlap them or they will stick together. Pour over the remaining sauce. Bake in a preheated oven, 180°C, 350°F, Gas Mark 4, for 20-25 minutes until the sauce is bubbling. Serve hot. No accompaniment is necessary.

Freezing: is recommended for the crespelle and the sauce before baking. Cover the baking dish with foil and overwrap in a freezer bag. This will keep for 2-3 months. Bake from frozen in a preheated oven, 180°C, 350°F, Gas Mark 4, still with the foil covering on, for about 40 minutes or until the sauce is bubbling and the crespelle are completely heated through.

SERVES 4

Nutritional content per serving:	Carbohydrate: 28 g	Fat: 17 g	Fibre: 3 g	Kilocalories: 340

Crespelle; Fusilli with Fresh Tomato and Basil Sauce

FUSILLI WITH FRESH TOMATO AND BASIL SAUCE

500 g (1 lb) ripe tomatoes, skinned and
    chopped finely
2 tablespoons olive oil
250-300 g (8-10 oz) fresh fusilli (pasta
    twists)
4-6 tablespoons double cream
6 basil leaves
65 g (2½ oz) freshly grated Parmesan cheese
salt and pepper

Put the tomatoes in a heavy pan with the oil and season to taste. Heat gently, stirring frequently, for 15 minutes. Meanwhile, bring a large pan of salted water to the boil. Add the pasta, stir and bring back to the boil. Reduce the heat slightly and boil, uncovered, for 3-4 minutes, or according to packet instructions, stirring occasionally.

Remove the sauce from the heat and stir in the cream. Tear half the basil into pieces and add to the sauce with half the Parmesan. Return to the lowest possible heat for 1-2 minutes, stirring. Drain the pasta and divide between 4 warm plates. Pour the sauce over. Garnish with the remaining cheese and basil and serve.

Freezing: is recommended for the sauce. Freeze in a rigid, airtight container. This will keep for up to 2 months. Defrost at room temperature for 2-3 hours, then reheat and complete the recipe.

SERVES 4

Nutritional content per serving: Carbohydrate: 20 g   Fat: 20 g   Fibre: 3 g   Kilocalories: 290

PAGLIA E FIENO WITH TOMATO AND ROSEMARY

FOR SAFETY'S SAKE, IT IS BEST TO REMOVE THE CHILLIES BEFORE SERVING!

600 g (1¼ lb) can of tomatoes
2 tablespoons olive oil
15 g (½ oz) butter
1 small carrot, chopped finely
1 small onion, chopped finely
1 celery stick, chopped finely
about 4 tablespoons red wine
2 whole dried red chillies
250-300 g (8-10 oz) fresh paglia e fieno (flat ribbon spinach and egg noodles, coiled into nests)
2 teaspoons chopped rosemary
salt and pepper
rosemary sprigs to garnish

Put the tomatoes and their juice in a blender and work to a purée. (Or simply push them through a sieve.)

Heat the oil and butter in a heavy saucepan. Add the carrot, onion and celery and cook gently, stirring frequently, until soft – about 15 minutes. Add the red wine, increase the heat and stir until the wine has been absorbed by the vegetables. Add the puréed tomatoes and the whole chillies. Season to taste. Bring to the boil. Reduce the heat, cover the pan and simmer for 15-20 minutes until the sauce is quite thick.

Meanwhile, bring a saucepan of salted water to the boil. Add the pasta, stir and bring back to the boil. Reduce the heat slightly and boil, uncovered, for 3-4 minutes, or according to packet instructions, stirring. Drain the pasta and turn it into a warm bowl. Remove the sauce from the heat and stir in the rosemary. Adjust the seasoning. Pour the sauce over the pasta and serve garnished with rosemary sprigs.

SERVES 4

Nutritional content per serving: Carbohydrate: 22 g   Fat: 11 g   Fibre: 3 g   Kilocalories: 210

Paglia e Fieno with Tomato and Rosemary

Pasta Shells with Guacamole Sauce

PASTA SHELLS WITH GUACAMOLE SAUCE

3 tablespoons olive oil

1 small onion, chopped finely

2 celery sticks, chopped finely

1 red or green pepper, cored, deseeded and
   diced finely

2 teaspoons chopped oregano or marjoram

½-1 teaspoon chilli powder, according to
   taste

1-2 garlic cloves, crushed

500 g (1 lb) ripe tomatoes, skinned, seeded
   and chopped, or 1 × 397 g (14 oz) can
   tomatoes, chopped with their juice

150 ml (¼ pint) dry white wine

230-300 g (8-10 oz) dried pasta shells

1 large ripe avocado

juice of ½ lemon

150 ml (¼ pint) soured cream or Greek
   yogurt

salt and pepper

marjoram sprigs to garnish

Heat the oil in a heavy saucepan. Add the onion, celery and diced pepper and cook gently, stirring frequently, until softened – about 10 minutes. Add the oregano or marjoram, chilli powder and garlic and stir over a gentle heat for 1-2 minutes until the ingredients are mixed.

Add the tomatoes and wine and season to taste. Stir well. Cover and simmer gently for 15 minutes, stirring occasionally.

Meanwhile, bring a large saucepan of salted water to the boil. Add the pasta, stir and bring back to the boil. Reduce the heat slightly and boil, uncovered, for 10 minutes or according to the packet instructions, stirring occasionally.

Halve, stone and peel the avocado. Dice the flesh and sprinkle it with the lemon juice (to prevent discoloration). Remove the sauce from the heat and stir in the avocado and half the soured cream or yogurt. Taste and adjust the seasoning if necessary.

Drain the pasta well and turn it into a warm bowl. Pour over the sauce and toss the sauce and pasta gently together to heat them through. Serve in warm soup plates, with the remaining soured cream or yogurt spooned on top. Garnish with sprigs of marjoram. No accompaniment is necessary.

SERVES 4

Nutritional content per serving: Carbohydrate: 57 g   Fat: 28 g   Fibre: 5 g   Kilocalories: 535

Chinese wonton

WONTON ARE LITTLE PARCELS MADE FROM A SIMPLE FLOUR AND WATER DOUGH. WHEN DEEP-FRIED, THE DOUGH BECOMES CRISP AND CRUNCHY, THE PERFECT WRAPPING FOR THE SOFT, SPICY CHICKEN AND HAM FILLING HIDDEN INSIDE

125 ml (4 fl oz) lukewarm water

150 g (5 oz) boneless cooked chicken, chopped finely or minced

100 g (3½ oz) cooked ham, chopped finely or minced

1 small onion, chopped very finely

2 tablespoons soy sauce

2 teaspoons ground ginger

sunflower oil, for deep frying

feuille de chêne or quattro staggione leaves to garnish

DOUGH:

200 g (7 oz) strong plain flour

salt

DIP:

2.5 cm (1 inch) piece fresh root ginger, peeled and chopped roughly

1-2 cloves garlic, according to taste, chopped roughly

1 tablespoon sesame oil

6 tablespoons soy sauce

1 tablespoon sesame seeds

First make the dough. Sift the flour and a pinch of salt into a bowl. Mix in the water with a fork until the dough starts to come together. Turn the dough out on to a floured surface and knead until smooth. Return the dough to the floured bowl, cover with a tea towel and leave to rest for 30 minutes.

Meanwhile, prepare the filling. Put the chicken and ham in a bowl, add the onion, soy sauce and ginger and mix with your hands until the ingredients are evenly combined. Cover and set aside.

To make the dip, pound the ginger and garlic in a mortar and pestle. Gradually whisk in the oil and soy sauce. Turn into a small serving bowl, cover and chill in the refrigerator until serving time.

Divide the dough in half. Roll out one half on a floured surface to form a long sausage and cut it into 8 equal pieces. Flatten each piece between the palms of your hands, then roll them out with a rolling pin to make eight 10-12 cm (4-5 inch) circles.

Hold 1 circle of dough in the palm of your hand and put about 1 tablespoon of the filling mixture in the centre. With the fingers of the other hand, gather the edges of the dough together over the filling, twisting them slightly to seal in the filling.

Heat the oil in a deep-fat fryer until it is hot but not smoking. Deep-fry the wonton for 2-3 minutes until they are light golden in colour. Remove them with a slotted spoon and drain on kitchen paper.

Repeat this process with the remaining dough and filling to make 16 wonton altogether. Serve them as soon as they are all made. Whisk the dip to amalgamate the ingredients again, sprinkle the sesame seeds on top and hand it separately. Garnish with feuille de chêne or quattro staggione leaves. No other accompaniment is necessary.

Freezing: is recommended. Open freeze the uncooked wonton until solid, then pack in freezer bags. These will keep for up to 1 month. Defrost at room temperature for about 4 hours, then continue as above.

SERVES 4-5

Nutritional content per serving: Carbohydrate: 47 g   Fat: 19 g   Fibre: 2 g   Kilocalories: 435

Chinese Wonton; Chinese-Style Vermicelli

CHINESE-STYLE VERMICELLI

250 g (8 oz) dried vermicelli
4 carrots, cut into fine julienne
4 courgettes, cut into fine julienne
125 g (4 oz) small mangetout, topped and
   tailed
2 tablespoons groundnut or corn oil
4 spring onions, sliced diagonally
2.5 cm (1 inch) piece fresh root ginger, peeled
   and sliced into thin matchstick strips
1-2 cloves garlic, crushed
4 tablespoons soy sauce
1 tablespoon clear honey
1 tablespoon wine vinegar
1 teaspoon coriander seeds, crushed
salt and pepper
parsley leaves to garnish

Bring a large saucepan of salted water to the boil. Add the vermicelli, stir and bring back to the boil. Reduce the heat slightly and boil, uncovered, for 8-10 minutes, or according to the packet instructions, stirring occasionally.

Meanwhile, put the carrots, courgettes and mangetout in a colander or sieve and sprinkle with salt to taste. Place the colander over the pan of boiling vermicelli. Cover the colander and steam until the vegetables are tender but still crunchy – this will take 5 minutes at the most. Remove the colander and set it aside. Drain the vermicelli well and cut it into shorter lengths with kitchen scissors.

Heat the oil in a wok or deep frying-pan. Add the spring onions and ginger and cook gently, stirring, until the ingredients give off a spicy aroma. Add the garlic, soy sauce, honey, wine vinegar and coriander seeds, stirring well. Add the vermicelli and vegetables. Increase the heat and toss the ingredients in the pan vigorously until they are evenly combined and very hot. Season with pepper to taste. Turn into a warm serving bowl and garnish with parsley leaves. Serve at once. No accompaniment is necessary.

SERVES 4

Nutritional content per serving: Carbohydrate: 65 g   Fat: 8 g   Fibre: 5 g   Kilocalories: 360

Spaghetti with Prawns and Vodka

3 tablespoons olive oil
1 small onion, chopped finely
1 × 225 g (8 oz) can tomatoes
1 clove garlic, crushed
3 tablespoons dry white wine (optional)
1 teaspoon tomato purée
a few sprigs of rosemary and basil leaves
250-300 g (8-10 oz) spaghetti
15 g (½ oz) butter
250 g (8 oz) peeled prawns, thoroughly
   defrosted and dried if frozen
1 × 300 g (10 oz) can whole button
   mushrooms, drained
4 tablespoons vodka
75 ml (3 fl oz) double cream
salt and pepper
TO GARNISH:
unpeeled prawns
basil leaves

Heat half the oil in a heavy pan. Add the onion and cook it gently, stirring frequently, until softened – about 5 minutes. Add the tomatoes and the garlic and stir the tomatoes well to break them up, pressing them against the side of the pan if necessary. Add the wine if used, the tomato purée, rosemary and basil leaves. Season to taste. Simmer, uncovered, for about 15 minutes, stirring until the sauce is reduced to a thick purée. Remove the pan from the heat. Bring a large pan of salted water to the boil. Add the spaghetti, stir and bring back to the boil. Reduce the heat slightly and boil, uncovered, for 10-12 minutes, or according to packet instructions, stirring occasionally.

Meanwhile, heat the remaining oil in a heavy frying pan. Add the butter and heat until it is sizzling. Add the prawns and mushrooms, stirring well. Pour in the vodka, increase the heat and cook, stirring constantly, until all the liquid has evaporated. Add the tomato sauce and cream and stir until well blended and heated through.

Drain the spaghetti well and transfer it to a warm bowl. Pour over the sauce, which should be a pretty pink colour and serve at once, garnished with a few unpeeled prawns and basil leaves.

Freezing: is recommended for the sauce. Freeze in a rigid, airtight container. This will keep for up to 2 months. Defrost at room temperature, then reheat and continue as above.

SERVES 4

Nutritional content per serving: Carbohydrate: 58 g   Fat: 22 g   Fibre: 4 g   Kilocalories: 570

Trenette with Mixed Herbs and Pine Kernels

50-65 g (2-2½ oz) mixed herbs, eg basil,
   parsley and sage
50 g (2 oz) pine kernels
2 cloves garlic, chopped roughly
90 ml (3½ fl oz) olive oil
250-300 g (8-10 oz) dried trenette or
   tagliatelle
4 tablespoons freshly grated Pecorino or
   Parmesan cheese
salt and pepper

Wash the herbs and pat them dry thoroughly with kitchen paper. Place them in a food processor. Add the pine kernels and garlic and chop very finely. Add the oil in a thin, steady stream, working the machine until a fine, creamy sauce is obtained.

Bring a large saucepan of salted water to the boil. Add the pasta, stir and bring back to the boil. Reduce the heat slightly and boil, uncovered, for 10 minutes, or according to the packet instructions, stirring occasionally. Transfer the sauce to a warm bowl. Add the cheese and season to taste. Stir well to blend. Drain the pasta. Add to the sauce and toss well to combine. Serve at once.

SERVES 4

Nutritional content per serving: Carbohydrate: 53 g   Fat: 34 g   Fibre: 3 g   Kilocalories: 580

Spaghetti with Prawns and Vodka; Trenette with Mixed Herbs and Pine Kernels

SICILIAN PASTA WITH SARDINES AND GARLIC

500 g (1 lb) fresh sardines
3 tablespoons olive oil
2 small onions, chopped finely
6 cloves garlic, crushed
250 g (8 oz) ripe tomatoes, skinned, seeded
  and finely chopped, or 1 × 227 g (8 oz)
  can tomatoes, chopped with their juice
4 canned anchovy fillets in oil, pounded to a
  purée with the oil from the can
6 black olives, pitted
1 tablespoon capers
1 tablespoon pine kernels
1 tablespoon chopped basil
250-300 g (8-10 oz) dried pasta shells
pepper

Remove the heads and tails from the sardines. Open the fish out gently with your fingers and remove the bones. (Do not worry if the fish breaks because it will break during cooking anyway.)

Heat the oil in a heavy saucepan. Add the onions and cook gently, stirring frequently, until they are golden – about 10 minutes. Add the sardines and garlic and stir to coat the sardines in the oil and onion. Add all the remaining ingredients, except the pasta. Cover the pan and cook gently for 10-15 minutes. Meanwhile, bring a large saucepan of salted water to the boil. Add the pasta, stir and bring back to the boil. Reduce the heat slightly and boil, uncovered, for 10 minutes, or according to packet instructions, stirring occasionally.

Drain the pasta well and divide it equally between 4 warm soup plates. Taste the sauce for seasoning, then pour it over the pasta and serve at once. Serve with Italian bread sticks and an Italian red wine.

SERVES 4

Nutritional content per serving: Carbohydrate: 60 g   Fat: 32 g   Fibre: 4 g   Kilocalories: 680

SPAGHETTI WITH ANCHOVIES

250-300 g (8-10 oz) spaghetti
3 × 50 g (2 oz) cans anchovies in oil
1 clove garlic, crushed
finely grated rind and juice of 1 orange
pinch of sugar
2 tablespoons freshly grated Parmesan cheese
2 tablespoons chopped mint
salt and pepper

Bring a large saucepan of salted water to the boil. Add the spaghetti, stir and bring back to the boil. Reduce the heat slightly and boil, uncovered, for 10-12 minutes, or according to the packet instructions, stirring occasionally. Meanwhile, drain the anchovy oil into a heavy saucepan and place over moderate heat until hot. Chop the anchovies roughly and add them to the pan with the garlic. Stir with a wooden spoon, pressing the anchovies so that they break up and become almost puréed. Add the orange rind and juice, the sugar and pepper to taste. Stir vigorously to heat through and combine with the anchovies.

Drain the spaghetti well and turn it into a warm serving bowl. Pour over the sauce, add the Parmesan and half the mint and toss together quickly. Serve at once, sprinkled with the remaining mint.

Microwave: Immerse the spaghetti in 1.2 litres (2 pints) boiling salted water in a bowl and cook on High Power for 10-12 minutes, stirring once. Cover and leave to stand while preparing the anchovies. Place the anchovies and oil in a bowl with the garlic and cook on High Power for 2 minutes, stirring once. Purée the mixture by beating with a spoon then add the orange rind and juice, sugar and pepper to taste. Drain the spaghetti and toss with the sauce, mint and Parmesan.

SERVES 4

Nutritional content per serving: Carbohydrate: 53 g   Fat: 10 g   Fibre: 2 g   Kilocalories: 375

Sicilian Pasta with Sardines and Garlic; Spaghetti with Anchovies; Pasta Alfredo

PASTA ALFREDO

THIS POPULAR DISH IS SIMPLICITY ITSELF – AND TAKES UNDER 10 MINUTES TO PREPARE

250-300 g (8-10 oz) fresh tagliatelle
25 g (1 oz) butter
150 ml (¼ pint) double cream
2 tablespoons finely chopped parsley
3 tablespoons freshly grated Parmesan cheese
salt and pepper

Bring a large saucepan of salted water to the boil. Add the tagliatelle, stir and bring back to the boil. Reduce the heat slightly and boil, uncovered, for 3-4 minutes, stirring occasionally.

Meanwhile, melt the butter in a small, heavy saucepan. Add the cream and parsley and heat through, stirring. Add the Parmesan with salt and pepper to taste and stir until the cheese has totally melted into the cream.

Drain the tagliatelle well and turn it into a warm serving bowl. Pour over the sauce and toss well to combine the sauce and pasta. Serve at once, with extra cheese handed separately if liked. No accompaniment is necessary, apart from a bottle of dry white wine.

SERVES 4

Nutritional content per serving: Carbohydrate: 17 g   Fat: 27 g   Fibre: 1 g   Kilocalories: 335

CANNELLONI WITH RICOTTA AND WALNUTS

THE SMOKED BACON IN THIS STUFFING ADDS A NICE TOUCH OF FLAVOUR, BUT IF YOU PREFER NOT TO USE MEAT, IT CAN EASILY BE OMITTED AND A FEW EXTRA WALNUTS ADDED INSTEAD

1 tablespoon olive oil
8 cannelloni tubes
50 g (2 oz) smoked streaky bacon, derinded and chopped finely
175 g (6 oz) ricotta or curd cheese
50 g (2 oz) shelled walnuts, chopped finely
50 g (2 oz) freshly grated Parmesan cheese
pinch of grated nutmeg
1 egg
50 g (2 oz) fresh breadcrumbs
vegetable oil for deep frying
salt and pepper

Bring a large saucepan of salted water to the boil. Swirl in the oil, then add half the cannelloni tubes and bring back to the boil. Reduce the heat slightly and boil, uncovered, for 3-4 minutes until the tubes are just pliable. Remove the cannelloni tubes with a slotted spoon and rinse them under cold running water to stop them cooking further. Leave the tubes to drain well on kitchen paper. Repeat with the remaining cannelloni.

Place the chopped bacon in a heavy saucepan and heat it gently until the fat runs. Cook until the bacon turns a darker colour and is fairly crisp. Remove the bacon with a slotted spoon and drain on kitchen paper.

Place the ricotta cheese in a bowl and beat it with a wooden spoon to soften it slightly. Add the bacon, walnuts, half the Parmesan cheese and the nutmeg and season with salt and pepper to taste. Beat the mixture well and use it to fill the cannelloni tubes, pushing the cheese mixture in with a teaspoon.

Beat the egg in a shallow dish with salt and pepper to taste. Combine the breadcrumbs on a plate with the remaining Parmesan. Dip the cannelloni first in the egg, then coat evenly with breadcrumbs and cheese. Chill the filled cannelloni tubes in the refrigerator for about 30 minutes.

Heat the oil in a deep-fat fryer until it is hot but not smoking. Deep-fry half the cannelloni for 2-3 minutes until they are golden brown. Remove with a slotted spoon and drain well on kitchen paper. Repeat with the remaining cannelloni. Serve as soon as the cannelloni are all made, with a mixed salad, and if you desire, a delicious homemade tomato sauce (see page 26).

SERVES 4

Nutritional content per serving: Carbohydrate: 40 g   Fat: 34 g   Fibre: 2 g   Kilocalories: 550

Cannelloni with Ricotta and Walnuts; Spaghetti with Clam Sauce

SPAGHETTI WITH CLAM SAUCE

1 × 397 g (14 oz) can tomatoes
4 tablespoons dry red or white wine
2 tablespoons finely chopped parsley
2 teaspoons finely chopped basil
2 tablespoons olive oil
1 small onion, chopped finely
2 cloves garlic, crushed
250-300 g (8-10 oz) spaghetti
1 × 290 g (9½ oz) can baby clams, well
  drained
salt and pepper
TO GARNISH:
chopped parsely
clams in their shells

Place the canned tomatoes with their juice in a blender or food processor. Add the wine and herbs and work to a purée.

Heat the oil in a heavy saucepan. Add the onion and fry gently, stirring frequently, until it has softened – about 5 minutes. Add the garlic and puréed tomatoes. Season with salt and pepper to taste. Cover and simmer gently for about 15 minutes, stirring occasionally.

Meanwhile, bring a large saucepan of salted water to the boil. Add the spaghetti, stir and bring back to the boil. Reduce the heat slightly and boil, uncovered, for 10-12 minutes, or according to the packet instructions, stirring occasionally.

Stir the clams into the tomato sauce and heat them through. Adjust the seasoning if necessary. Drain the spaghetti well and turn it into a warm serving bowl. Pour over the sauce and garnish with chopped parsley and clams in their shells. Serve at once.

SERVES 4

Nutritional content per serving: Carbohydrate: 59 g   Fat: 9 g   Fibre: 4 g   Kilocalories: 335

FAMILY MEALS

NUTRITIOUS, INEXPENSIVE, FILLING AND TASTY — PASTA IS THE PERFECT CHOICE IF YOU'RE CATERING FOR A HUNGRY FAMILY. IT'S QUICK TO PREPARE AND COOK TOO, MAKING IT AN ABSOLUTE MUST FOR MIDWEEK MEALS. PASTA, IN ALL SHAPES, SIZES AND COLOURS, IS SURE TO BECOME A REGULAR FAMILY FAVOURITE.

SPAGHETTI WITH EGG AND BACON SAUCE

DO NOT WORRY THAT THE EGGS ARE NOT COOKED IN THE SAUCE – THE HEAT OF THE PASTA COOKS THEM SUFFICIENTLY

375-425 g (12-14 oz) dried spaghetti

4 eggs (size 1 or 2)

4 tablespoons freshly grated Parmesan cheese

4 tablespoons cream or top of the milk

2 tablespoons olive oil

1 small onion, chopped finely

6 rashers smoked streaky bacon, derinded and
cut into short strips

1 clove garlic, crushed

salt and pepper

Bring a large pan of salted water to the boil. Add the pasta, stir and bring back to the boil. Reduce the heat and boil, for 10-12 minutes, or according to packet instructions, stirring occasionally.

Meanwhile, beat the eggs in a bowl with the grated Parmesan and cream or milk. Season to taste with salt and pepper and set aside.

Heat the oil in a separate, large heavy saucepan. Add the onion and cook gently, stirring until it has softened – about 5 minutes. Add the bacon and cook, stirring, until it changes colour; stir in the garlic.

Drain the spaghetti well and turn it into the saucepan with the bacon. Toss over a moderate heat to combine the ingredients. Remove the pan from the heat and add the egg mixture. Toss to coat each strand of spaghetti with the sauce. Divide the spaghetti equally between 4 warm soup plates and serve at once.

SERVES 4

Nutritional content per serving: Carbohydrate: 76 g   Fat: 31 g   Fibre: 3 g   Kilocalories: 675

MACARONI WITH FOUR CHEESES

200 g (7 oz) dried short-cut macaroni

1 teaspoon olive oil

65 g (2½ oz) butter

50 g (2 oz) plain flour

600 ml (1 pint) milk

75 g (3 oz) Gruyère cheese, grated

1 teaspoon French mustard

65 g (2½ oz) grated Mozzarella cheese

65 g (2½ oz) Dolcelatte cheese, diced

6 tablespoons freshly grated Parmesan
cheese

1 tablespoon dried wholemeal breadcrumbs

salt and pepper

Bring a large saucepan of salted water to the boil, add the macaroni and the oil and bring back to the boil. Stir, reduce the heat slightly and boil, uncovered, for 8-10 minutes or according to packet instructions.

Meanwhile, melt 50 g (2 oz) of the butter in a heavy saucepan. Add the flour and cook, stirring, for 1 minute. Gradually blend in the milk. Bring it the boil, still stirring, and simmer for 3 minutes. Add the Gruyère and season with salt and pepper to taste. Stir until the cheese has melted. Remove the pan from the heat and stir in the mustard.

Drain the macaroni well. Cover the bottom of a 1.2 litre (2 pint) baking dish with a few tablespoons of the sauce. Put half of the macaroni in the dish, spreading it out in an even layer, then add a layer made up of half of the Mozzarella, Dolcelatte and Parmesan. Pour over half of the remaining sauce. Repeat the layers with the remaining macaroni, Mozzarella and Dolcelatte. Pour over the remaining sauce. Sprinkle the remaining Parmesan and the breadcrumbs on top and dot with the remaining butter. Bake in a preheated oven 180°C, 350°F, Gas Mark 4 for 20 minutes or until the cheese is bubbling and golden on top. Serve hot with a salad of radicchio, dressed with a fresh vinaigrette.

SERVES 4

Nutritional content per serving: Carbohydrate: 62 g   Fat: 35 g   Fibre: 3 g   Kilocalories: 660

Spaghetti with Egg and Bacon Sauce; Macaroni with Four Cheeses

Pasta twists with ratatouille sauce

MAKE THIS VEGETABLE SAUCE AT THE END OF SUMMER, WHEN RATATOUILLE VEGETABLES ARE AT THEIR FRESHEST AND BEST – AND MOST ECONOMICAL. IF YOU HAPPEN TO HAVE WINE OPEN, UP TO 150 ML (¼ PINT) OF DRY WHITE WINE CAN BE USED INSTEAD OF STOCK

1 aubergine, cut lengthways into thin strips
2½ tablespoons olive oil
1 onion, sliced thinly
1 red pepper, cored, deseeded and halved lengthways
1 yellow pepper, cored, deseeded and halved lengthways
500 g (1 lb) ripe tomatoes, skinned and chopped roughly
2 cloves garlic, crushed
2 tablespoons tomato purée
2 teaspoons chopped basil or parsley
pinch of sugar, or to taste
300-450 ml (½-¾ pint) vegetable stock
375 g (12 oz) dried wholewheat pasta twists
salt and pepper
chopped parsley to garnish

Put the aubergine strips in a colander, sprinkling them with salt. Press a plate on top of the strips and weight it down. Leave the aubergines for 20 minutes to remove the bitter taste (dégorgé).

Meanwhile, heat 2 tablespoons of the oil in a heavy saucepan. Add the onion and cook gently, stirring frequently, until it has softened – about 5 minutes. Cut the peppers lengthways into thin strips, add them to the pan and cook gently for 5 minutes. Add the tomatoes and garlic, stirring well. Rinse the aubergines under cold running water to remove the salt and bitter juices. Add them to the pan with the tomato purée, herbs and sugar. Season with salt and pepper to taste. Bring to the boil, stirring. Reduce the heat, cover the pan and simmer gently for 20 minutes. Add the stock gradually, to dilute the sauce as it thickens, and to prevent the vegetables sticking to the bottom of the pan.

Meanwhile, bring a large saucepan of salted water to the boil, add the pasta twists and the remaining oil and bring back to the boil. Reduce the heat slightly and boil, uncovered, for 15 minutes, or according to the packet instructions, stirring occasionally.

Drain the pasta twists well and turn them into a warm serving bowl. Taste the sauce and adjust the seasoning if necessary. Pour the sauce over the pasta. Top with parsley and a sprinkling of Parmesan and serve at once, with extra Parmesan handed separately in a bowl. Serve with wholemeal bread, for a nutritious vegetarian meal.

Freezing: is recommended for the sauce. Freeze in a rigid, airtight container. This will keep for up to 3 months. Defrost in a refrigerator overnight or at room temperature for 4-6 hours then reheat until bubbling.

Microwave: Prepare the aubergine as above. Place the oil in a bowl and cook on High Power for 1 minute. Add the onion, cover and cook on High Power for 3 minutes, stirring once. Add the pepper, tomatoes, garlic, aubergine, purée, herbs and seasoning. Cover and cook on High Power for 8 minutes, stirring once. Add half the amount of stock required for the conventional cooking method, cover and cook on High Power for a further 6 minutes. Place the pasta in a bowl with 1.8 litres (3 pints) boiling water. Cook on High Power for 10 minutes, stirring once. Leave to stand, covered, for 3 minutes then drain. Place in a bowl and pour over the sauce.

SERVES 4

Nutritional content per serving: Carbohydrate: 67 g   Fat: 13 g   Fibre: 12 g   Kilocalories: 420

Pasta Twists with Ratatouille Sauce; Farfalle with Tuna, Tomato and Black Olives

FARFALLE WITH TUNA, TOMATO AND BLACK OLIVES

DO NOT ADD SALT TO THE SAUCE UNTIL YOU HAVE TASTED IT, JUST BEFORE SERVING – ANCHOVIES AND OLIVES ARE SALTY AND YOU MAY FIND THAT NO ADDED SALT IS NECESSARY

3 tablespoons olive oil

1 clove garlic, chopped roughly

1 × 50 g (2 oz) can anchovies in olive oil, drained and chopped roughly

500 g (1 lb) ripe tomatoes, skinned and chopped finely, or 1 × 397 g (14 oz) can tomatoes, chopped finely with their juice

2 teaspoons chopped mixed herbs (basil, oregano, parsley, marjoram)

375-425 g (12-14 oz) dried farfalle (pasta bows)

1 × 198 g (7 oz) can tuna in soya or vegetable oil, drained and flaked

1 × 99 g (3½ oz) can tuna in soya or vegetable oil, drained and flaked

16 black olives, pitted

salt and pepper

chopped parsley to garnish

Heat 2 tablespoons of the oil in a heavy saucepan. Add the garlic and fry gently until it is golden brown. Remove the garlic from the oil with a slotted spoon and discard it. Add the anchovies and stir, pressing the anchovies so that they break up and become almost puréed.

Add the tomatoes and bring to the boil, stirring. Reduce the heat and add the herbs with pepper to taste. Cover the pan and simmer for 15-20 minutes, stirring occasionally. Meanwhile, bring a large saucepan of salted water to the boil, add the farfalle, stir and bring back to the boil. Reduce the heat slightly and boil, uncovered, for 8-10 minutes, or according to the packet instructions, stirring occasionally.

Drain the farfalle well and turn it into a warm bowl. Pour over the remaining olive oil and toss the farfalle to coat them evenly. Stir the tuna and olives gently into the sauce, and heat through.

Pour half of the sauce over the farfalle in the bowl and toss the pasta and sauce together. Divide the mixture equally between 4 warm soup plates and spoon the remaining sauce on top. Garnish each serving with chopped parsley and serve at once.

SERVES 4

Nutritional content per serving: Carbohydrate: 77 g   Fat: 30 g   Fibre: 5 g   Kilocalories: 685

Spaghetti bolognese

2 tablespoons olive oil
1 carrot, chopped finely
1 onion, chopped finely
2 celery sticks, chopped finely
4 rashers smoked streaky bacon, derinded and
  chopped finely
375-500 g (12 oz-1 lb) minced beef
2 cloves garlic, crushed
150 ml (¼ pint) red wine
2 × 397 g (14 oz) cans tomatoes
2 teaspoons dried mixed herbs
1 teaspoon dried oregano or basil
375-425 g (12-14 oz) spaghetti
salt and pepper
oregano sprigs to garnish

Heat the oil in a heavy saucepan. Add the carrot, onion, celery and bacon and cook gently, stirring frequently, until the vegetables are soft. Add the minced beef and garlic and cook until the meat has changed colour, stirring all the time with a wooden spoon and pressing the meat against the side of the pan to remove all lumps. Add the wine, the tomatoes with their juice and the herbs. Season to taste. Bring to the boil, stirring. Reduce the heat, cover the pan and simmer gently for 45 minutes to 1 hour, stirring occasionally until the sauce is thick.

About 20 minutes before the end of cooking the sauce, bring a large saucepan of salted water to the boil. Add the spaghetti, stir and bring back to the boil. Reduce the heat and boil, uncovered, for 10-12 minutes or according to the packet instructions, stirring occasionally.

Drain the spaghetti well and turn it into a warm serving bowl. Pour the sauce over the spaghetti. Garnish with oregano sprigs. Serve at once.

Freezing: is recommended for the sauce. Freeze in a rigid, airtight container. This will keep for up to 3 months. Defrost overnight in a refrigerator or at room temperature for 4-6 hours then reheat until bubbling. Continue as above.

SERVES 4

Nutritional content per serving:	Carbohydrate: 85 g	Fat: 22 g	Fibre: 6 g	Kilocalories: 650

Conchiglie with chick peas and tahini

2 tablespoons olive oil
2 cloves garlic, crushed
2 × 397 g (14 oz) cans chick peas
2 tablespoons tahini paste
2 tablespoons finely chopped parsley
juice of ½ lemon, or to taste
375-425 g (12-14 oz) dried large conchiglie
  (pasta shells)
salt and pepper

Heat the oil in a heavy pan, add the garlic and fry very gently until it is just beginning to change colour. Drain the chick peas and pour 4 tablespoons of the liquid into the pan. Add the chick peas, the tahini paste, half of the parsley, the juice of ½ lemon, salt and pepper and ½ pint (300 ml) cold water. Bring slowly to the boil, stirring, and simmer for 10 minutes. Meanwhile, bring a pan of salted water to the boil. Add the pasta, stir and bring to the boil. Reduce the heat and boil, for 10 minutes or according to packet instructions, stirring occasionally.

Transfer the chick pea mixture to a blender and blend it to a purée. (If you do not have a machine, push the mixture through a sieve.) Rinse out the pan, return the purée to it and heat it through. If the sauce is a little too thick, add a few tablespoons of water until it is the right consistency for pouring over pasta. Adjust seasoning.

Drain the pasta well and turn into a warm bowl. Add the sauce and toss together gently. Serve garnished with the remaining parsley.

SERVES 4

Nutritional content per serving:	Carbohydrate: 120 g	Fat: 19 g	Fibre: 15 g	Kilocalories: 715

Spaghetti Bolognese; Conchiglie with Chick Peas and Tahini; Spaghetti with Tomatoes and Bacon

SPAGHETTI WITH TOMATOES AND BACON

375 g (12 oz) smoked streaky bacon, derinded
  and cut into 1 cm (½ inch) strips
1 onion, chopped finely
625 g (1¼ lb) ripe tomatoes, skinned and
  chopped roughly, or 1 × 397 g (14 oz) can
  and 1 × 227 g (8 oz) can tomatoes,
  chopped with their juice
375-425 g (12-14 oz) spaghetti
salt and pepper

Put the bacon into a heavy pan and place it over a moderate heat until the fat runs. Add the onion and cook for 10-15 minutes, stirring, until the bacon is almost crisp and the onions are soft and golden. Add the tomatoes and plenty of pepper, stirring to combine with the bacon and onion. Bring to the boil, stirring. Reduce the heat, cover the pan and simmer for 20 minutes, stirring occasionally. Meanwhile, boil a large pan of salted water. Add the pasta, stir and bring back to the boil. Reduce the heat and boil, uncovered, for 10-12 minutes, or according to packet instructions, stirring occasionally.

Drain the spaghetti well and turn it into a warm bowl. Pour the sauce over the spaghetti and serve, sprinkled with a little Parmesan.

Freezing: is recommended for the sauce. Freeze in a rigid, airtight container. This will keep for up to 1 month. Defrost in a refrigerator overnight, or at room temperature for 4-6 hours. Reheat gently until completely heated through. Continue as above.

SERVES 4

Nutritional content per serving: Carbohydrate: 80 g   Fat: 35 g   Fibre: 5 g   Kilocalories: 720

Spaghetti supreme

200 g (7 oz) dried spaghetti, broken into
    short lengths
1 × 198 g (7 oz) can sweetcorn kernels
about 400 ml (14 fl oz) milk
25 g (1 oz) butter
1 small onion, chopped finely
200 g (7 oz) boneless chicken breast, skinned
    and cut into 1 cm (½ inch) dice
25 g (1 oz) plain flour
1 × 300 g (10.6 oz) can whole button
    mushrooms, drained
2 tablespoons finely chopped parsley
50 g (2 oz) grated Mozzarella or Cheddar
    cheese
salt and pepper

Bring a pan of salted water to boil. Add the pasta, stir and bring back to the boil. Reduce the heat and boil, for about 10 minutes. Drain the corn and make the liquid up to 450 ml (¾ pint) with milk. Melt the butter in a pan. Add the onion and cook, stirring until soft.

Add the chicken and stir-fry for 5-8 minutes until just cooked. Add the flour and cook, stirring, for 1 minute. Gradually blend in the milk, bring to the boil, still stirring, and simmer for 3 minutes. Drain the spaghetti and add to the sauce with the corn, mushrooms and parsley. Season to taste. Fold the ingredients until mixed. Transfer to a shallow 1.2 litre (2 pint) flameproof dish. Level and sprinkle on the cheese. Place under a hot grill for about 5 minutes until bubbling on top. Serve with a salad, tossed in a dressing made with lemon juice.

SERVES 4

Nutritional content per serving: Carbohydrate: 61 g   Fat: 11 g   Fibre: 7 g   Kilocalories: 450

Vegetable lasagne

3 tablespoons olive oil
1 large onion, sliced thinly
3 peppers (1 red, 1 green and 1 yellow),
    cored, deseeded and cut into thin
    lengthways strips
500 g (1 lb) button mushrooms, sliced thinly
1-2 cloves garlic, according to taste, crushed
2 tablespoons chopped mixed herbs (basil,
    chives, parsley, rosemary, thyme)
50 g (2 oz) butter
50 g (2 oz) plain flour
900 ml (1½ pints) milk
175 g (6 oz) Vegetarian Cheddar cheese,
    grated
1 quantity Bolognese Sauce (see page 42)
    made without bacon or beef
12 sheets 'no pre-cook' wholewheat lasagne
salt and pepper

Heat the oil in a heavy pan. Add the onion and peppers and cook gently, stirring occasionally, until they are soft – about 10-15 minutes. Put in a bowl and set aside. Add the mushrooms and garlic to the pan and toss over high heat until the mushrooms are coloured. Remove from the heat and stir in the herbs. Add to the peppers and season.

Melt the butter in a pan. Add the flour and cook, stirring, for 1 minute. Gradually blend in the milk, bring to the boil, stirring and simmer for 3 minutes. Add 125 g (4 oz) of the Cheddar and season to taste. Stir until the cheese has melted. Remove from the heat. Pour a third of the tomato sauce into a baking dish measuring about 28 × 23cm (11 × 9 inches). Cover with a third of the mushroom mixture and arrange 4 sheets of lasagne in a layer on top. Pour over a third of the cheese sauce and repeat these 4 layers twice, ending with the sauce. Sprinkle on the remaining cheese. Place in a preheated oven 190°C, 375°F, Gas Mark 5 for 40 minutes or until bubbling on top.

Freezing: is recommended before baking. Cover the baking dish with foil and overwrap in a freezer bag. This will keep for up to 3 months. Bake from frozen in a preheated oven, 190°C, 375°F, Gas Mark 5, still with the foil covering on, for about 50 minutes or until bubbling.

SERVES 6

Nutritional content per serving: Carbohydrate: 73 g   Fat: 29 g   Fibre: 9 g   Kilocalories: 635

Spaghetti Supreme; Vegetable Lasagne; Mee Goreng

MEE GORENG

THIS QUICKLY PREPARED SINGAPOREAN DISH CONTAINS TOFU (BEAN CURD), WHICH IS AN EXCELLENT SOURCE OF LOW-FAT PROTEIN

250 g (8 oz) thread egg noodles
4 tablespoons groundnut or corn oil
250 g (8 oz) firm tofu (bean curd), drained
  and cut into cubes
1 small onion, chopped finely
3 cloves garlic, crushed
1 fresh red chilli, chopped finely, or
  ½ teaspoon chilli powder
4 celery sticks, sliced thinly
1 bunch spring onions, cut into
  5 cm (2 inch) lengths
175 g (6 oz) Chinese leaves, shredded
2-3 tablespoons soy sauce
salt and pepper
TO GARNISH:
2 eggs, beaten
½ cucumber, cut into short, thin strips

Bring a large saucepan of water to the boil. Add the noodles, cover the pan and immediately remove it from the heat. Leave to stand for 6 minutes. Drain thoroughly. Heat 2 tablespoons of the oil in a wok or deep, heavy frying-pan. Add the tofu and stir-fry over a moderate heat for 2-3 minutes, taking care not to break the pieces up. Lift the tofu out carefully, drain it on kitchen paper and keep warm.

Add 1 tablespoon of oil to the pan and heat until hot but not smoking. Add the onion, garlic and chilli and stir-fry until they are softened – about 2-3 minutes. Add the celery and stir-fry for 2 minutes. Add the spring onions and Chinese leaves and stir-fry for 1 further minute. Add the noodles and soy sauce and season with salt and pepper to taste. Toss the ingredients together over a high heat until they are thoroughly heated through. Return the tofu to the pan and carefully combine it with other ingredients. Heat the remaining oil in a heavy frying-pan. Pour in the beaten eggs and make an omelette. Slide the omelette on to a board and cut it into strips. Transfer the mee goreng into a warm bowl and garnish with the omelette and cucumber.

SERVES 4

Nutritional content per serving: Carbohydrate: 50 g   Fat: 19 g   Fibre: 4 g   Kilocalories: 420

FUSILLI WITH CHICKEN AND ROSEMARY

50 g (2 oz) butter
1 small onion, chopped finely
250 g (8 oz) white button mushrooms, sliced
  thinly
2 cloves garlic, crushed
1½ tablespoons plain flour
250 ml (8 fl oz) chicken stock
500-750 g (1-1½ lb) boneless chicken
  breasts, skin removed and cut on the
  diagonal into thin strips
4 tablespoons medium dry sherry
2 teaspoons chopped rosemary
375-425 g (12-14 oz) dried fusilli (pasta
  twists)
150 ml (¼ pint) double cream
salt and pepper
rosemary sprigs to garnish

Melt the butter in a pan. Add the onion and cook gently, stirring—about 5 minutes. Add the mushrooms and garlic and stir over a moderate heat until the juices run. Remove the mushrooms and set aside.

Add the flour to the juices and cook, stirring, for 1 minute. Gradually blend in the stock, and bring to the boil, stirring. Simmer for 3 minutes. Reduce the heat and add the chicken, sherry and rosemary. Season to taste. Cover and simmer for 15 minutes, stirring occasionally. Meanwhile, bring a pan of salted water to the boil. Add the fusilli, and bring to the boil. Reduce the heat and boil, for 8-10 minutes, or according to packet instructions, stirring occasionally.

Remove the sauce from the heat and stir in the cream and mushrooms. Return to the lowest heat for 1-2 minutes, stirring.

Drain the fusilli well and turn into a warm bowl. Pour over the sauce. Serve at once, garnished with rosemary.

SERVES 4

Nutritional content per serving: Carbohydrate: 80 g   Fat: 35 g   Fibre: 5 g   Kilocalories: 820

TAGLIATELLE WITH SPICY SAUSAGE SAUCE

2 tablespoons olive oil
1 onion, chopped finely
4 cloves garlic, crushed
1 × 397 g (14 oz) can tomatoes and
  1 × 227 g (8 oz) can tomatoes, chopped
  with their juice
125 g (4 oz) frozen petits pois
375-425 g (12-14 oz) fresh tagliatelle
200 g (7 oz) spicy salami sausage, skin
  removed and finely diced
2 tablespoons finely chopped parsley
salt and pepper

Heat the oil in a heavy pan. Add the onion, stirring until soft. Add the garlic and tomatoes and bring to the boil, stirring. Reduce the heat, cover and simmer for 20 minutes, adding the petits pois halfway. Meanwhile, bring a large pan of salted water to the boil. Add the pasta, stir and bring back to the boil. Reduce the heat and boil, for 3-4 minutes or according to packet instructions, stirring occasionally.

Add the salami and parsley to the sauce and heat for 3-4 minutes. Drain the pasta and divide between 4 plates. Pour over the sauce.

Microwave: Place the oil in a bowl and cook on High Power for 1 minute. Add the onion, cover and cook on High Power for 3 minutes. Add the garlic and tomatoes, re-cover and cook on High Power for 5 minutes. Add the petits pois, re-cover and cook on High Power for a further four minutes. Place the pasta in a bowl with 1.2 litres (2 pints) boiling salted water and cook on High Power for 3 minutes. Leave to stand, covered, for 2 minutes. Meanwhile, add the salami and parsley to the sauce and cook on High Power for 1-2 minutes to reheat. Drain the pasta and serve with the sauce as above.

SERVES 4

Nutritional content per serving: Carbohydrate: 9 g   Fat: 20 g   Fibre: 6 g   Kilocalories: 360

Fusilli with Chicken and Rosemary; Tagliatelle with Spicy Sausage Sauce

CHICKEN AND MACARONI 'PIE'

200 g (7 oz) dried short-cut macaroni
2 tablespoons olive oil
2 onions, chopped finely
200 g (7 oz) boneless chicken breast, skinned
and cut into 5 mm (¼ inch) dice
200 g (7 oz) button mushrooms, quartered
3 tablespoons chopped parsley
25 g (1 oz) butter
25 g (1 oz) plain flour
450 ml (¾ pint) milk
125 g (4 oz) grated Mozzarella cheese
pinch of chilli powder
2 eggs, beaten
6 tablespoons dried wholemeal breadcrumbs
salt and pepper

Bring a large pan of salted water to the boil. Add the macaroni and half the oil and bring back to the boil. Stir, reduce the heat and boil, for 8-10 minutes or according to packet instructions. Drain well.

Heat the remaining oil in a heavy saucepan. Add the onions and cook over a moderate heat, stirring frequently, until they are golden – about 5 minutes. Add the diced chicken and stir-fry for 5 minutes. Add the mushrooms and continue cooking for a further 5 minutes. Remove from the heat. Stir in the parsley and season with salt and pepper.

Melt the butter in a small heavy saucepan. Add the flour and cook, stirring, for 1 minute. Gradually blend in the milk, and bring to the boil, still stirring. Simmer for 3 minutes. Add the Mozzarella, chilli powder and salt and pepper to taste. Stir the sauce until the cheese has melted. Remove the pan from the heat and leave the sauce to cool slightly. Stir in first the beaten eggs and then the macaroni.

Brush the inside of a 20 cm (8 inch) spring-form cake tin liberally with butter. Coat it evenly with 4 tablespoons of the breadcrumbs.

Pour half the macaroni mixture into the tin and level the surface. Spoon the chicken mixture on top and cover with the remaining macaroni. Smooth and sprinkle with the remaining breadcrumbs.

Bake the 'pie' in a preheated oven 190°C, 375°F, Gas Mark 5 for 35 minutes, or until it feels set in the centre when pressed. Remove from the oven and allow to stand for 10 minutes. Loosen the side of the tin and slide the 'pie' on to a warm serving plate. Serve hot, with a plain tomato sauce and a salad.

Microwave: Place the pasta, half the oil and 1.2 litres (2 pints) boiling water in a bowl and cook on High Power for 10 minutes, stirring once. Cover and leave to stand. Place the remaining oil in a bowl and cook on High Power for 1 minute. Add the onions, cover and cook on High Power for 6 minutes, stirring once. Add the chicken and cook on High Power for 3 minutes. Add the mushrooms and cook on High Power for 2 minutes. Stir in the parsley and seasoning. Place the butter in a bowl and cook on High Power for 1 minute. Stir in the flour and gradually add the milk. Cook on High Power for 4-6 minutes, until boiling and thickened, stirring 3 times. Add the Mozzarella, chilli and season to taste. Prepare a 20 cm (8 inch) deep cake tin and spoon in the macaroni and chicken mixture as above. Sprinkle with the remaining breadcrumbs and cook on High Power for 5 minutes. Reduce the power to Medium and cook for 10-14 minutes or until firm in the centre.

SERVES 4-6

Nutritional content per serving: Carbohydrate: 60 g   Fat: 22 g   Fibre: 6 g   Kilocalories: 560

Chicken and Macaroni 'Pie'; Cannelloni with Tuna and Peas

CANNELLONI WITH TUNA AND PEAS

24 'no pre-cook' cannelloni tubes
25 g (1 oz) Parmesan cheese, freshly grated
FILLING:
50 g (2 oz) butter
50 g (2 oz) plain flour
300 ml (½ pint) milk
75 g (3 oz) Danish Svenbo or Gruyère cheese,
   grated
½ teaspoon ground paprika
2 × 198 g (7 oz) cans tuna, drained and
   flaked
175 g (6 oz) frozen petits pois
salt and pepper
SAUCE:
25 g (1 oz) butter
40 g (1½ oz) plain flour
900 ml (1½ pints) milk
50 g (2 oz) Danish Svenbo or Gruyère cheese,
   grated

Make the filling. Melt the butter in a heavy pan, add the flour and cook, stirring, for 1 minute. Gradually blend in the milk, bring to the boil, still stirring, and simmer for 3 minutes. Stir constantly as the sauce is very thick. Transfer the sauce to a bowl and stir in the grated cheese and paprika. Season to taste. Fold in the tuna and peas until they are mixed. Fill the tubes with this mixture, and set them aside. Rinse the pan and make the sauce as for the filling. Add the cheese and season to taste. Stir until the cheese has melted.

Cover the bottom of a baking dish, measuring about 35 × 25cm (14 × 10 inches) with a little sauce. Arrange the tubes in the dish side by side in a single layer and cover with the remaining sauce. Sprinkle over the Parmesan. Place in a preheated oven, 190°C, 375°F, Gas Mark 5 for 30-40 minutes or until bubbling and golden on top. Serve hot.

SERVES 4-6

Nutritional content per serving: Carbohydrate: 46 g   Fat: 55 g   Fibre: 9 g   Kilocalories: 1130

SPAGHETTI WITH MEATBALLS

500 g (1 lb) minced beef
½ large onion, chopped very finely
1 clove garlic, crushed
1 teaspoon chopped oregano
1 teaspoon dried mixed herbs
50 g (2 oz) fresh breadcrumbs
1 egg, beaten
2 tablespoons olive oil
375-425 g (12-14 oz) dried spaghetti
salt and pepper
parsley sprigs to garnish
SAUCE:
1 onion
1 × 397 g (14 oz) can tomatoes
600 ml (1 pint) beef stock
2 tablespoons tomato purée
1 tablespoon red wine vinegar
1 teaspoon chopped oregano
1 teaspoon dried mixed herbs
1 teaspoon sugar

Put all the sauce ingredients in a blender and work to a purée. Transfer to a pan and season. Bring to the boil, stirring. Reduce the heat, cover and simmer stirring occasionally while making the meatballs.

Place the beef in a bowl and combine it with the onion, garlic, herbs, breadcrumbs and egg. Season to taste. Knead for about 5 minutes until the meat is sticky. Shape into about 50 <u>very small</u> balls.

Heat the oil in a non-stick frying pan and fry the meatballs in batches for 5-7 minutes until they are brown on all sides. Remove them and place them on kitchen paper to drain. Add the meatballs to the sauce. Cover the pan and cook very gently for about 20 minutes, shaking the pan occasionally. Bring a large pan of salted water to the boil. Add the spaghetti, stir and bring back to the boil. Reduce the heat slightly and boil, uncovered, for 10-12 minutes, stirring occasionally.

Drain the spaghetti and transfer it to a warm bowl. Pour a few spoonfuls of the sauce over the spaghetti, combine it well. Divide the spaghetti equally between warm soup plates. Place the meatballs on top and spoon over the remaining sauce. Garnish with parsley sprigs.

Freezing: is recommended for the sauce and the meatballs. Freeze in an airtight container. These will keep for up to 3 months. Defrost in a refrigerator overnight or at room temperature for 4-6 hours. Reheat until the sauce is bubbling and meatballs are heated through.

SERVES 4-6

Nutritional content per serving: Carbohydrate: 93 g   Fat: 22 g   Fibre: 6 g   Kilocalories: 700

Spaghetti with Meatballs

Chap-Chee

CHAP-CHEE

THIS KOREAN SPECIALITY COMBINES MEAT AND VEGETABLES IN ONE DISH. IF YOU HAVE TIME, FREEZE THE MEAT FOR 30 MINUTES TO 1 HOUR BEFORE CUTTING. WHEN MEAT IS HALF-FROZEN IT IS VERY EASY TO SLICE PAPER-THIN

375 g (12 oz) fillet or rump steak, trimmed of fat and cut across the grain into thin strips
125 g (4 oz) thread egg noodles
3 tablespoons groundnut or corn oil
1 small onion, sliced thinly
2 carrots, cut into fine strips
125 g (4 oz) button mushrooms, sliced
125 g (4 oz) Chinese leaves, shredded
125 g (4 oz) spinach leaves, torn into pieces
salt and pepper
chopped spring onion tops to garnish
MARINADE:
2 tablespoons soy sauce
1 tablespoon groundnut oil
1 tablespoon sesame seeds
1 teaspoon soft brown sugar
1 spring onion, chopped finely
1 cm (½ inch) piece fresh root ginger, peeled and crushed
1-2 cloves garlic, crushed

First make the marinade. Mix all the ingredients together in a bowl. Add the beef strips and turn them over to coat them thoroughly. Cover and leave to marinate in a cool place for about 30 minutes.

Bring a large saucepan of water to the boil. Add the noodles, cover the pan and immediately remove from the heat. Leave to stand for 6 minutes. Drain the noodles and cut them into 5-7 cm (2-3 inch) lengths with kitchen scissors.

Heat the oil in a wok or deep, heavy frying-pan. Add the beef and marinade and stir-fry over a brisk heat for about 5 minutes until the meat is tender but still pink in the centre. Remove the meat from the pan with a slotted spoon and set it aside. Reduce the heat, add the onion and stir-fry until it has softened and is light golden. Add the carrots and stir-fry for 3-4 minutes. Add the mushrooms, Chinese leaves and spinach and stir-fry for 1-2 minutes more. Finally return the beef to the pan, and add the noodles. Increase the heat to maximum and toss the ingredients together to heat them through. Season with salt and pepper to taste. Turn into a warm serving bowl, sprinkle over the chopped spring onion tops and serve at once. No accompaniment is necessary.

SERVES 4

Nutritional content per serving: Carbohydrate: 31 g   Fat: 28 g   Fibre: 4 g   Kilocalories: 495

LASAGNE AL FORNO

THIS IS A NORTHERN ITALIAN VERSION OF THE EVER-POPULAR LASAGNE, WHICH INCLUDES MEATBALLS AND CHOPPED HARD-BOILED EGGS AMONG ITS MANY DELICIOUS LAYERS. A CARTON OF READY-MADE BOLOGNESE SAUCE IS USED TO SAVE TIME

450 ml (¾ pint) milk
1 small onion, sliced
1 bay leaf
1 bouquet garni (sprig each of parsley, thyme and rosemary)
250 g (8 oz) minced beef
5 tablespoons freshly grated Parmesan cheese
3 tablespoons chopped parsley
1 clove garlic, crushed
40 g (1½ oz) plain flour
1 tablespoon olive oil
25 g (1 oz) butter
pinch of grated nutmeg
1 × 350 g (12.3 oz) carton Bolognese Sauce
125 ml (4 fl oz) beef stock or red wine
12 sheets 'no pre-cook' lasagne verde
2 hard-boiled eggs, shelled and chopped roughly
salt and pepper
bay leaves to garnish

Put the milk, onion, bay leaf and bouquet garni in a saucepan over a moderate heat. As soon as the milk comes to the boil, remove the pan from the heat, cover it and leave the milk to infuse for about 20 minutes.

Place the minced beef in a bowl with 2 tablespoons of the Parmesan cheese, the parsley and garlic. Season with salt and pepper to taste. Knead with your hands for about 5 minutes until the meat is sticky, then shape it into 24 small balls. Roll the meatballs in 15 g (½ oz) of the flour. Heat the oil in a non-stick frying pan and fry the meatballs in batches for 5-7 minutes until they are brown on all sides. Remove with a slotted spoon and drain on kitchen paper.

To make a béchamel sauce, strain the infused milk. Melt the butter in a heavy saucepan, add the remaining flour and cook, stirring, for 1 minute. Gradually blend in the milk. Bring to the boil, still stirring, and simmer for 3 minutes. Season to taste with nutmeg, salt and pepper and remove the pan from the heat.

Mix the Bolognese sauce with the stock or wine. Pour a thin layer of this sauce into a baking dish measuring about 28 × 23 cm (11 × 9 inches). Arrange 4 sheets of lasagne in a single layer on top, then pour over half the remaining Bolognese sauce. Place the meatballs in an even layer in the dish and sprinkle with the chopped hard-boiled eggs. Arrange 4 more sheets of lasagne in the dish and pour over the remaining Bolognese sauce. Cover with the remaining 4 sheets of lasagne, coat with the béchamel sauce and sprinkle the remaining Parmesan evenly on top.

Place in a preheated oven 200°C, 400°F, Gas Mark 6 and bake for 35 minutes or until bubbling and golden brown on top. Serve hot, straight from the dish, garnished with bay leaves. Serve with a green salad tossed in a sharp vinaigrette dressing.

Freezing: is recommended before baking. Cover the baking dish with foil and overwrap in a freezer bag. This will keep for up to 3 months. Bake from frozen in a preheated oven, 200°C, 400°F, Gas Mark 6, still with the foil covering on, for about 50 minutes or until bubbling and heated through. Remove the foil to brown if necessary.

SERVES 6

Nutritional content per serving: Carbohydrate: 64 g   Fat: 27 g   Fibre: 3 g   Kilocalories: 590

Lasagne al Forno; Pasta with Spring Vegetables

PASTA WITH SPRING VEGETABLES

200 g (7 oz) broccoli florets, divided into
   tiny sprigs
4 young carrots, sliced thinly
200 g (7 oz) frozen petits pois
375 g (12 oz) dried penne (pasta quills)
25 g (1 oz) butter
200 g (7 oz) small button mushrooms,
   quartered
6 tablespoons dry white wine
2 tablespoons finely chopped parsley
300 ml (½ pint) soured cream
6 tablespoons freshly grated Parmesan
   cheese
salt and pepper

Cook the broccoli and carrots in boiling salted water for 5-7 minutes until they are tender but still crunchy. Remove with a slotted spoon and drain. Add the petits pois to the water and bring back to the boil. Simmer for 3-4 minutes. Drain well.

Bring a large saucepan of salted water to the boil. Add the penne, stir and bring back to the boil. Reduce the heat and boil, uncovered, for 10 minutes or according to packet instructions, stirring occasionally.

Melt the butter in a heavy saucepan. Stir in the mushrooms, wine and parsley and season. Cook for 8-10 minutes, stirring. Add the vegetables and toss over a high heat to heat through.

Drain the penne thoroughly and turn them into a warm bowl. Add the soured cream, vegetables and 4 tablespoons of the Parmesan and toss them quickly together. Divide the pasta equally between 4 warm soup plates. Sprinkle the remaining Parmesan on top and serve at once.

SERVES 4

Nutritional content per serving: Carbohydrate: 53 g   Fat: 9 g   Fibre: 8 g   Kilocalories: 350

PERSIAN PRAWN EGGAH

AN EGGAH IS A KIND OF THICK, FLAT OMELETTE, NOT UNLIKE THE SPANISH TORTILLA

1.4 litres (2½ pints) chicken stock
125 g (4 oz) medium egg noodles
3 tablespoons groundnut or corn oil
250 g (8 oz) peeled cooked prawns, defrosted
  and thoroughly dried if frozen
2 teaspoons tomato purée
2 teaspoons ground cumin
¼-½ teaspoon chilli powder, according to
  taste
1 tablespoon chopped coriander
4 eggs
1 large onion, sliced thinly
1 teaspoon ground paprika
salt and pepper

Bring the stock to the boil in a large saucepan. Add the noodles, cover the pan and immediately remove it from the heat. Leave to stand for 6 minutes. Heat 1 tablespoon of the oil in a wok or deep heavy frying-pan. Add the prawns, tomato purée, cumin and chilli powder. Season to taste with salt and pepper and stir-fry over a brisk heat for 2-3 minutes until the prawns are evenly coated. Remove the pan from the heat, stir in the chopped coriander and set aside.

Drain the noodles well and cut them into short lengths with kitchen scissors. Beat the eggs lightly in a large bowl. Add the prawn mixture and noodles, stirring well.

Heat the remaining oil in a large, heavy frying pan. Add the onion and paprika and cook gently, stirring frequently, until the onion has softened. Pour in the egg mixture and stir so that the ingredients are evenly mixed in the pan. Cook for 15-20 minutes, then slide the eggah on to a plate. Return the eggah to the pan, turning it over to cook the other side. Cook for a further 15 minutes. Serve hot with a mixed salad.

SERVES 4

Nutritional content per serving: Carbohydrate: 25 g   Fat: 20 g   Fibre: 3 g   Kilocalories: 375

RIGATONI WITH CHICKEN LIVERS AND HERBS

50 g (2 oz) butter
250 g (8 oz) button mushrooms, sliced
2-3 cloves garlic, according to taste, crushed
1 tablespoon finely chopped thyme
1 tablespoon finely chopped sage
375-425 g (12-14 oz) dried rigatoni or penne
250 g (8 oz) chicken livers, trimmed and cut
  into small dice
4 tablespoons medium dry sherry
salt and pepper

Melt half the butter in a heavy frying-pan. Add the mushrooms, garlic and herbs and season with salt and pepper to taste. Cook gently, stirring occasionally, for 10 minutes.

Bring a large saucepan of salted water to the boil, add the rigatoni, stir and bring back to the boil. Reduce the heat and boil, uncovered, for 10 minutes, or according to packet instructions, stirring occasionally.

Remove the mushrooms from the frying-pan with a slotted spoon and set them aside on a plate. Melt the remaining butter in the pan and add the diced chicken livers. Fry them briskly over a high heat for about 5 minutes until the pieces are tender but still pink and juicy in the centre. Return the mushrooms to the pan, with any juices that have collected on the plate, and the sherry. Toss the ingredients together and adjust the seasoning if necessary. Drain the pasta and turn into a warm bowl. Pour over the liver mixture and combine the pasta and sauce. Serve at once.

SERVES 4

Nutritional content per serving: Carbohydrate: 75 g   Fat: 15 g   Fibre: 4 g   Kilocalories: 535

Persian Prawn Eggah; Rigatoni with Chicken Livers and Herbs; Mexican Pasta

MEXICAN PASTA

3 tablespoons olive oil

1 small onion, chopped finely

375 g (12 oz) minced beef

1 clove garlic, crushed

1 teaspoon chilli powder, or to taste

1 × 397 g (14 oz) can chopped tomatoes

2 tablespoons tomato purée

300 ml (½ pint) beef stock

2 teaspoons chopped oregano

250 g (8 oz) dried pasta wheels

1 × 213 g (7.5 oz) can red kidney beans, drained and well-rinsed

2 eggs, beaten

300 ml (½ pint) Greek yogurt

1 tablespoon freshly grated Parmesan cheese

salt and pepper

Heat 2 tablespoons of the oil in a flameproof casserole. Add the onion and fry until soft. Add the beef, garlic and chilli and cook until the meat changes colour, stirring and pressing the meat to remove lumps. Add the tomatoes, purée, stock and oregano and seasoning. Bring to the boil, stirring. Reduce the heat, cover and simmer gently for 20 minutes. Bring a pan of salted water to boil. Add the pasta and the remaining oil, stir and bring back to the boil. Reduce the heat and boil, for 10 minutes. Drain the pasta and mix into the sauce with the beans. Level the surface. Beat the eggs into the yogurt, and season. Pour the egg mixture over the pasta. Sprinkle with cheese and bake in a preheated oven, 180°C, 350°F, Gas Mark 4 for 45 minutes, until golden.

Freezing: is recommended for the sauce (without the beans). Freeze in a rigid, airtight container. This will keep for up to 3 months. Defrost overnight or at room temperature for 4-6 hours, then reheat until bubbling. Continue as above.

SERVES 6

Nutritional content per serving: Carbohydrate: 43 g   Fat: 27 g   Fibre: 2 g   Kilocalories: 485

PASTICCIO

THIS PIE IS AN UNUSUAL COMBINATION OF SWEET PASTRY, SAVOURY MEAT AND MACARONI.

4 teaspoons olive oil
1 onion, chopped finely
2 celery sticks, chopped finely
1 carrot, chopped finely
125 g (4 oz) chicken livers, trimmed and
  chopped
375 g (12 oz) minced beef
1 × 99 g (3.5 oz) tube tomato purée
450 ml (¾ pint) beef stock
2 tablespoons finely chopped parsley
1 teaspoon dried oregano
1 teaspoon dried mixed herbs
175 g (6 oz) dried short-cut macaroni
25 g (1 oz) Parmesan cheese, freshly grated
1 × 150 g (5 oz) packet Mozzarella cheese,
  drained and diced
½ egg white, lightly beaten, to glaze
salt and pepper
PASTRY:
300 g (10 oz) plain flour
pinch of salt
150 g (5 oz) caster sugar
75 g (3 oz) butter or lard, or a mixture of
  both, cut into small pieces
1 whole egg
1 egg yolk

First make the pastry. Sift the flour and salt into a large bowl and stir in the sugar. Add the pieces of fat to the flour and rub them in with the fingertips until the mixture resembles fine breadcrumbs. Add the egg and egg yolk and mix with a fork to make a smooth dough. Turn the dough out on to a floured surface. Knead it lightly until smooth and use two thirds to line the bottom and sides of a 20 cm (8 inch) spring-form cake tin. Place in the refrigerator to chill while making the filling.

Heat 3 teaspoons of the oil in a heavy pan. Add the onion and cook gently, stirring until it has softened – about 5 minutes. Add the celery and carrot and cook, stirring, for a further 5 minutes. Add the livers and beef. Cook until the beef has changed colour, stirring all the time, pressing the meat against the pan to remove all lumps. Add the purée, stock and herbs and season to taste. Bring to the boil, stirring. Reduce heat, cover and simmer gently for 20 minutes.

Bring a large saucepan of salted water to the boil and swirl in the remaining oil. Add the macaroni, stir and bring back to the boil. Reduce the heat and boil, uncovered, for 8-10 minutes, or according to the packet instructions, stirring occasionally. Drain the macaroni well and turn it into a large bowl. Strain the juices from the meat sauce into the macaroni. Add the Parmesan cheese, stirring well. Leave both the meat sauce and the macaroni mixture to cool. Put half the macaroni mixture into the pastry-lined tin and level the surface. Spoon in the cold meat sauce and dot with the Mozzarella. Cover with the remaining macaroni. Roll out the remaining pastry on a floured surface and use to make a pie lid, patching up any cracks by sticking them together with water. Press the edges of the pastry together to make a firm seal. Press the tines of a fork around the edge and make a few slits in the top. Brush the pastry with egg white to glaze. Place the pie in a preheated oven, 190°C, 375°F, Gas Mark 5 for 25 minutes. Reduce the temperature to 160°C, 325°F, Gas Mark 3, and bake for a further 25 minutes or until the pastry is golden brown. Remove from the oven and allow to stand for 10 minutes. Loosen the side of the tin and slide the pasticcio on to a warm plate. Serve hot with a crisp green salad.

SERVES 6

Nutritional content per serving: Carbohydrate: 98 g   Fat: 44 g   Fibre: 4 g   Kilocalories: 890

Pasticcio; Pasta Parmigiana

PASTA PARMIGIANA

125 ml (4 fl oz) olive oil
200 g (7 oz) dried wholewheat pasta shapes
2 aubergines, cut into 5 mm (¼ inch) slices
4 tablespoons freshly grated Parmesan cheese
125 g (4 oz) Mozzarella cheese, sliced thinly
salt and pepper
marjoram sprigs to garnish
SAUCE:
1 tablespoon olive oil
1 onion, chopped finely
1-2 cloves garlic, according to taste, crushed
1 × 397 g (14 oz) can tomatoes
250 ml (8 fl oz) vegetable stock or water
1 bay leaf
1 sprig basil, parsley or mint

To make the sauce, heat the oil in a pan. Add the onion and cook until soft. Add the other ingredients, season and bring to the boil, breaking up the tomatoes by mashing against the pan. Cover and simmer for 20 minutes. Bring a pan of salted water to the boil and add 1-2 teaspoons of oil. Add the pasta, stir and bring to the boil. Reduce the heat and boil, for 10 minutes, until half-cooked. Drain. Fry the aubergines in batches until golden, then drain.

Put half the pasta in a layer in a 5 cm (2 inch) deep baking dish measuring about 28 × 23 cm (11 × 9 inches). Cover with half the aubergines, a third of the sauce and a third of the Parmesan. Repeat the layers. Cover the top with Mozzarella and the remaining Parmesan. Place in a preheated oven, 190°C, 375°F, Gas Mark 5, for 30-35 minutes until bubbling. Serve garnished with marjoram.

Freezing: is recommended before baking. Cover the baking dish with foil and overwrap in a freezer bag. This will keep for up to one month. Bake from frozen in a preheated oven, 190°C, 375°F, Gas Mark 5, still with the foil covering, for about 50 minutes or until bubbling and completely heated through. Remove foil to brown if necessary.

SERVES 4

Nutritional content per serving: Carbohydrate: 39 g   Fat: 47 g   Fibre: 8 g   Kilocalories: 570

SPECIAL OCCASIONS

FOR ENTERTAINING, NOTHING BEATS PASTA — EVERYBODY LOVES IT! — QUICK TO PREPARE AND EASY TO EAT, IT'S THE IDEAL PARTY FOOD TO SHARE WITH A CROWD. MANY OF THE DISHES IN THIS CHAPTER CAN BE PREPARED IN ADVANCE, TAKING ALL THE STRAIN OUT OF SPECIAL OCCASIONS.

TORTELLINI ALLA BOLOGNESE

ALTHOUGH TORTELLINI ARE SERVED AS A STARTER, YOU CAN USE THEM AS A MAIN DISH BY ADDING BOLOGNESE SAUCE (SEE PAGE 42)

25 g (1 oz) butter
50 g (2 oz) pork, minced finely
50 g (2 oz) veal, minced finely
25 g (1 oz) boiled ham, chopped finely
50 g (2 oz) Mozzarella cheese, diced
3 tablespoons freshly grated Parmesan cheese
1 tablespoon finely chopped parsley
1 egg yolk
grated nutmeg
salt and pepper
parsley sprigs to garnish
PASTA DOUGH:
200 g (7 oz) plain flour
¼ teaspoon salt
2 eggs
1 tablespoon olive oil, for cooking
TO SERVE:
melted butter
Parmesan cheese

Make the filling. Melt the butter in a frying pan add the pork and veal and cook, stirring, for 5-10 minutes until the meat has changed colour. Transfer to a bowl and leave to cool, stirring from time to time to prevent the butter sinking to the bottom. Add the remaining filling ingredients and season with nutmeg, salt and pepper. Stir well to obtain a sticky mixture. Set the filling aside.

To make the dough, sift the flour and salt into a bowl. Mix in the eggs. Knead, roll, cut out, fill and cook as for Tortellini with Cream (see page 60). When the tortellini are cooked, divide them between 4-6 warm plates. Drizzle over melted butter and sprinkle grated Parmesan on top. Serve, garnished with parsley sprigs.

Microwave: To make the filling, place the butter in a bowl and cook on High Power for 1 minute. Add the pork and veal and cook on High Power for 2½-3 minutes. Leave to cool as above. Add the remaining filling ingredients and seasoning. Prepare the pasta as above filling with the mixture. Place in a bowl with 1.2 litres (2 pints) boiling salted water and cook on High Power for 3-4 minutes. Drain and serve as above.

SERVES 4-6

Nutritional content per serving: Carbohydrate: 40 g Fat: 21 g Fibre: 2 g Kilocalories: 430

CONCHIGLIE WITH GORGONZOLA AND WALNUTS

WALNUTS HAVE A TENDENCY TO DISCOLOUR ANY SAUCE, SO DON'T ADD THEM UNTIL THE LAST MOMENT, JUST AT THE POINT OF SERVING

250-300 g (8-10 oz) dried conchiglie (pasta shells)
25 g (1 oz) butter
250 g (8 oz) ricotta or curd cheese
250 g (8 oz) Gorgonzola or Dolcelatte cheese, rind removed, mashed
about 4 tablespoons milk
1 teaspoon chopped sage
125 g (4 oz) shelled walnuts, chopped finely
salt and pepper
chopped sage to garnish

Bring a large saucepan of salted water to the boil. Add the pasta, stir and bring back to the boil. Reduce the heat and boil, uncovered, for 10 minutes or according to the packet instructions, stirring occasionally.

Melt the butter in a heavy saucepan, add the ricotta or curd cheese and remove from the heat. Beat well with a wooden spoon until the cheese has melted. Add the mashed Gorgonzola, return the pan to a very gentle heat and continue stirring until the cheese has melted. Stir in enough milk to give a thick, pouring consistency. Season with sage and pepper. (Do not add salt as the Gorgonzola is very salty.)

Drain the pasta well and turn it into a warm bowl. Add the sauce and the walnuts and toss them together. Divide equally between 4 warm soup plates and garnish with chopped sage. Serve at once.

SERVES 4 as a starter

Nutritional content per serving: Carbohydrate: 55 g Fat: 42 g Fibre: 4 g Kilocalories: 590

Conchiglie with Gorgonzola and Walnuts; Tortellini alla Bolognese

TORTELLINI WITH CREAM

ALTHOUGH TRADITIONALLY SERVED AS A STARTER, THIS RICH AND CREAMY DISH OF TORTELLINI STUFFED WITH CHICKEN AND HAM WOULD ALSO BE GOOD FOR A LIGHT LUNCH OR SUPPER DISH SERVED WITH A LEAFY SALAD OF FRISÉE OR ESCAROLE, FEUILLE DE CHÊNE OR QUATTRO STAGIONI AND RADICCHIO TOSSED IN A VINAIGRETTE DRESSING. IF YOU CAN GET SOME FRESH NASTURTIUM FLOWERS AND LEAVES TO GARNISH, THE SALAD WILL LOOK EXCEPTIONALLY PRETTY

75 g (3 oz) cooked chicken breast, chopped finely
75 g (3 oz) boiled ham, chopped finely
1 egg, beaten
2 tablespoons freshly grated Parmesan cheese
grated nutmeg
a little medium dry sherry or dry white wine, to moisten
150 ml (¼ pint) double cream
salt and pepper
PASTA DOUGH:
200 g (7 oz) strong plain flour
¼ teaspoon salt
2 eggs, beaten
1 tablespoon olive oil, for cooking

Make the filling. Mix the chicken and ham in a bowl with the egg and Parmesan cheese and season with nutmeg and salt and pepper to taste. Moisten with a little sherry or wine if the filling seems too dry. Cover the bowl and set it aside.

Make the pasta dough. Sift the flour and salt into a bowl and mix in the eggs. Turn the dough out on to a floured surface and knead with floured hands until it is shiny and smooth – about 10 minutes. Cut the dough into quarters and wrap 3 pieces in a damp tea towel. Roll out the unwrapped piece until it is paper thin. Cut it into long strips 6 cm (2½ inches) wide. Using a pastry cutter or a glass, cut out 20 circles, each one 5 cm (2 inches) in diameter, re-rolling the trimmings as necessary.

Put a pea-sized ball of the filling in the centre of 1 circle, brush all round the edge with water. Fold the dough over to make a semi-circle in which the top and bottom edges do not quite meet. Press the edges together with a little water to seal them. Pull the 2 corners of the semi-circle around your index finger and press them together with a little water to seal. Place on a floured tea towel. Repeat with the remaining 19 circles, and continue rolling and cutting out the remaining dough, filling and shaping the tortellini until there are 80 altogether. Leave all the tortellini to dry out for about 30 minutes, turning them over once.

Bring a large saucepan of salted water to the boil, swirl in the olive oil, and add a batch of the tortellini. Stir and bring back to the boil, reduce the heat and boil, uncovered, for 1-2 minutes. Remove the cooked tortellini from the water with a slotted spoon, taking great care not to break them. Keep them hot while cooking the remainder.

Place all the tortellini in a warm bowl. Pour over the cream and season to taste with nutmeg, salt and pepper. Stir gently to coat them evenly with cream, and divide equally between 4-6 warm soup plates. Sprinkle with Parmesan and serve at once.

SERVES   4-6 as a starter, light lunch or supper

Nutritional content per serving: Carbohydrate: 41 g   Fat: 30 g   Fibre: 2 g   Kilocalories: 510

Tortellini with Cream; Farfalle with Spinach and Prawns

FARFALLE WITH SPINACH AND PRAWNS

HOT PASTA COMBINED WITH COLD PRAWNS AND RAW SPINACH MAKE AN UNUSUAL 'WARM SALAD', A QUICK AND EASY STARTER FOR A DINNER PARTY. FOR A SPECIAL TREAT, GARNISH THE SIDE OF EACH DISH WITH ONE OR TWO UNPEELED PRAWNS, THE LARGER THE BETTER

500 g (1 lb) peeled cooked prawns, defrosted
and thoroughly dried if frozen
375 g (12 oz) dried farfalle (pasta bows)
250 g (8 oz) spinach leaves, washed, dried
and torn into pieces
salt
MARINADE:
1 tablespoon coriander seeds
6 tablespoons olive oil
3-4 cloves garlic, crushed
2 tablespoons dry white wine
2 tablespoons Pernod
finely grated rind and juice of 1 lime
salt and pepper

First make the marinade. Dry fry the coriander seeds in a non-stick frying pan for a few seconds until they give off a spicy aroma. Transfer them to a mortar and crush finely with a pestle. Place in a large bowl with the remaining marinade ingredients. Whisk well to mix them together.

Stir the prawns into the marinade, coating them well. Cover and leave to marinate in a cold place for 3-4 hours, stirring occasionally.

Bring a large saucepan of salted water to the boil. Add the farfalle, stir and bring back to the boil. Reduce the heat and boil, for 8-10 minutes, or according to packet instructions, stirring occasionally.

Drain the farfalle well and turn them into a warm bowl. Add the prawns and marinade and toss them together well. Add the spinach and toss again. Adjust the seasoning if necessary. Divide the pasta equally between 8 warm soup plates and serve at once.

SERVES 8 as a starter

Nutritional content per serving:	Carbohydrate: 39 g	Fat: 13 g	Fibre: 2 g	Kilocalories: 355

CANNELLONI WITH BEEF AND CHICKEN LIVERS

25 g (1 oz) butter

2 tablespoons olive oil

1 onion, chopped finely

1 carrot, chopped finely

1 celery stick, chopped finely

500 g (1 lb) minced beef

125 g (4 oz) chicken livers

3 tablespoons tomato purée

1 × 227 g (8 oz) can tomatoes, chopped with
their juice

6 tablespoons medium dry sherry

2 tablespoons chopped parsley

2 tablespoons chopped basil

200 ml (7 fl oz) beef stock

50 g (2 oz) boiled ham, chopped finely

300 ml (½ pint) double cream

7 tablespoons freshly grated Parmesan cheese

salt and pepper

PASTA DOUGH:

200 g (7 oz) strong plain flour

¼ teaspoon salt

2 eggs, beaten

1 tablespoon olive oil, for cooking

First make the filling. Melt the butter with the oil in a heavy pan. Add the onion, carrot and celery and cook gently, stirring frequently, until the vegetables are soft – about 15 minutes. Add the beef and chicken livers and cook until the meat has changed colour, stirring all the time and pressing the meat against the pan to remove all lumps. Add the purée, tomatoes and the sherry. Season to taste. Bring to the boil, stirring. Reduce the heat, cover and simmer very gently for about 40 minutes, stirring occasionally.

Add the herbs and stock, cover and cook again for 10 minutes. Adjust the seasoning. Turn the mixture into a bowl and leave it to cool.

Make the pasta. Sift the flour and salt into a bowl, and mix in the eggs. Turn the dough out on to a floured surface and knead with floured hands until it is smooth and shiny – about 10 minutes.

Roll out the dough until it is paper thin and cut out 20 × 10 cm (4 inch) squares. Place them in a single layer on a floured tea towel. Do not overlap the edges or they will stick together.

Bring a large saucepan of salted water to the boil and swirl in the olive oil. Drop in a few pasta squares. Boil for 2-3 minutes, stirring all the time, until they are *al dente*. Remove them with a slotted spoon and replace them on the tea towel while cooking the remainder.

Take the chicken livers out of the sauce. Chop them finely and place them in a clean bowl with the ham. Remove the beef from the sauce, add it to the bowl and stir the meats together well.

Place the sauce in a clean pan and stir in the cream. Add 3 tablespoons of the grated Parmesan and simmer over a moderate heat for about 10 minutes until it has thickened slightly. Pour one third of the sauce into a baking dish measuring at least 25 × 20 cm (10 × 8 inches). Place 1 pasta square on a board and put about 1½ tablespoons of the mixture on half of the square. Roll up the pasta around the filling. Place the roll in the dish, seam side down. Repeat with the remaining pasta squares and filling, arranging them side by side in a single layer. Pour the remaining sauce over the cannelloni and sprinkle the remaining Parmesan on top. Bake in a preheated oven 190°C, 375°F, Gas Mark 5 for about 20 minutes or until the cheese is bubbling. Serve hot.

Freezing: is recommended before baking. Cover the baking dish with foil and overwrap in a freezer bag. This will keep for up to 3 months. Bake from frozen, in a preheated oven, 190°C, 375°F, Gas Mark 5, still with the foil covering on, for about 40 minutes or until the sauce is bubbling and the cannelloni are completely heated through.

SERVES   4-6 as a main course

Nutritional content per serving: Carbohydrate: 55 g   Fat: 62 g   Fibre: 5 g   Kilocalories: 970

Cannelloni with Beef and Chicken Livers; Farfalle with Mushrooms and Anchovies

FARFALLE WITH MUSHROOMS AND ANCHOVIES

As this sauce is quite delicate, make sure to buy the tiniest white button mushrooms you can find. Larger, darker mushrooms will discolour the sauce and spoil its pretty appearance

250-300 g (8-10 oz) dried farfalle (pasta
  bows)
25 g (1 oz) butter
2 tablespoons olive oil
500 g (1 lb) tiny white button mushrooms
2 cloves garlic, crushed
1 × 50 g (2 oz) can anchovies in oil,
  drained and chopped roughly
6 tablespoons chopped parsley
300 ml (½ pint) soured cream
salt and pepper

Bring a large saucepan of salted water to the boil. Add the pasta, stir and bring back to the boil. Reduce the heat and boil, uncovered, for 10 minutes or according to the packet instructions, stirring occasionally.

Melt the butter with the oil in a heavy saucepan. Add the mushrooms and garlic and fry over a moderate heat, stirring constantly, for 5 minutes until juices flow from the mushrooms.

Add the anchovies and season with pepper to taste. Cook for a further 5 minutes. Remove the pan from the heat and stir in 4 tablespoons of the parsley.

Drain the pasta well and turn it into a warm bowl. Add the sauce and cream and toss them gently together. Divide equally between 4 warm soup plates, sprinkle with the remaining parsley and serve.

SERVES 4

Nutritional content per serving: Carbohydrate: 55 g   Fat: 32 g   Fibre: 6 g   Kilocalories: 565

TORTELLONI WITH SPINACH AND RICOTTA

500 g (1 lb) fresh spinach, stalks removed
200 g (7 oz) ricotta or curd cheese
grated nutmeg
50 g (2 oz) butter
3 tablespoons finely chopped sage
3 tablespoons freshly grated Parmesan
  cheese
salt and pepper
sage leaves to garnish
PASTA DOUGH:
200 g (7 oz) strong plain flour
¼ teaspoon salt
2 eggs, beaten
1 tablespoon olive oil, for cooking

To make the filling, wash the spinach and place in a large saucepan with only the water clinging to the leaves. Cover and cook over a gentle heat for about 8 minutes or until tender. Drain well and leave to cool. Squeeze out the excess water with your hands.

Chop the spinach finely and place it in a bowl with the ricotta. Season with nutmeg, salt and pepper to taste. Beat the ingredients together well, cover and set aside.

Make the pasta dough. Sift the flour and salt into a bowl and mix in the eggs. Turn the dough out on to a floured surface and knead with floured hands until it is shiny and smooth – about 10 minutes.

Cut the dough into quarters and wrap 3 pieces in a damp tea towel. Roll out the unwrapped piece until it is paper thin. Using a pastry cutter or a glass, cut out 10 circles, each 7 cm (3 inches) in diameter, rerolling the trimmings as necessary.

Put 1 heaped teaspoon of filling in the centre of 1 circle and brush all round the edge with water. Fold the dough over to form a semi-circle, stretching the dough slightly if necessary. Press the edges together with a little water to seal. Pull the 2 corners of the semi-circle around your index finger, press them together with a little water to seal, and fold the sealed edges outwards. Place on a floured tea towel. Repeat with the remaining 9 circles, and continue rolling and cutting out the remaining dough, filling and shaping the tortelloni until there are 40 altogether. Leave all of the tortelloni to dry out for about 30 minutes, turning them over once.

Bring a large saucepan of salted water to the boil, swirl in the olive oil, and add a batch of tortelloni. Stir and bring back to the boil. Reduce the heat and boil, uncovered, for 1-2 minutes. Remove the cooked tortelloni from the water with a slotted spoon, taking great care not to break them. Keep them hot while cooking the remainder.

Melt the butter in a separate pan. Add the sage and fry it until crisp. Arrange the tortelloni in 4-6 warm soup plates. Drizzle over the sage butter and sprinkle sage leaves and grated Parmesan cheese on top. Serve at once as a starter with extra Parmesan cheese handed separately at the table. No other accompaniment is necessary.

SERVES   4-6 as a starter

Nutritional content per serving:	Carbohydrate: 44 g	Fat: 26 g	Fibre: 2 g	Kilocalories: 480

Tortelloni with Spinach and Ricotta; Tagliatelle Soufflé

TAGLIATELLE SOUFFLÉ

THIS IS NOT A TRUE SOUFFLÉ, WHICH SHOULD BE LIGHT, AIRY AND PUFFED UP. THE WEIGHT OF THE PASTA OBVIOUSLY PRODUCES A MORE 'PUDDINGY' RESULT, BUT IT'S DELICIOUS ALL THE SAME

250 g (8 oz) fresh tagliatelle verde
butter for greasing
75 g (3 oz) butter
50 g (2 oz) plain flour
300 ml (½ pint) milk
2 × 50 g (2 oz) cans anchovies in oil, drained and chopped
50 g (2 oz) Parmesan cheese, freshly grated
3 egg yolks
¼-½ teaspoon chilli powder, according to taste
6 egg whites
pepper

Bring a large saucepan of boiling water to the boil. Add the tagliatelle, stir and bring back to the boil. Reduce the heat and boil, uncovered, for 1 minute, just to soften and moisten the pasta slightly. Drain it well and cut into 5-7 cm (2-3 inch) lengths with kitchen scissors.

Butter the inside of a 1.4 litre (3 pint) soufflé dish or baking dish.

Melt the butter in a heavy saucepan, add the flour and cook, stirring, for 1 minute. Gradually blend in the milk, bring to the boil, still stirring and simmer for 3 minutes. Remove the pan from the heat, add the anchovies and all but 1 tablespoon of the Parmesan. Beat in the egg yolks and tagliatelle and season with chilli powder and pepper to taste.

Whisk the egg whites until they form stiff peaks. Fold in one third of the soufflé mixture, to slacken it slightly. Fold in the remaining egg whites and turn the mixture into the prepared dish. Sprinkle the remaining Parmesan on top and bake in a preheated oven 190°C, 375°F, Gas Mark 5 for 40 minutes or until golden brown. Serve hot, straight from the dish.

SERVES 6 as a starter or light lunch

Nutritional content per serving: Carbohydrate: 44 g   Fat: 18 g   Fibre: 2 g   Kilocalories: 400

CANNELLONI WITH CHICKEN AND HAM

300 g (10 oz) boneless chicken breasts,
  skinned
1 bunch of herbs (thyme, rosemary, tarragon,
  marjoram, parsley)
1 bay leaf
1 onion slice
250 g (8 oz) boiled ham
25 g (1 oz) butter with herbs and garlic
250 g (8 oz) button mushrooms, sliced
2 × 227 g (8 oz) packets frozen chopped
  spinach
25 g (1 oz) butter
25 g (1 oz) plain flour
150 ml (¼ pint) dry white wine
150 ml (¼ pint) double cream
1 × 227 g (8 oz) packet 'no pre-cook'
  cannelloni tubes
175 g (6 oz) Gruyère cheese, grated
salt and pepper
herb sprigs to garnish

Put the chicken in a pan with 450 ml (¾ pint) water, the herbs, bay leaf and onion and bring to the boil. Reduce the heat, cover and poach for 15 minutes. Lift out the chicken and strain the stock into a measuring jug. Mince the chicken and ham. Melt the herb and garlic butter in a heavy pan. Add the mushrooms and cook gently for 5 minutes, stirring. Add the spinach, cover and cook until just defrosted, breaking it up from time to time. Season the mixture and spread it out in a baking dish measuring about 28 × 23 cm (11 × 9 inches). Melt the plain butter in the rinsed-out pan. Add the flour and cook, stirring, for 1 minute. Gradually blend in 300 ml (½ pint) of the stock, then the wine and the cream. Bring to the boil, stirring, and simmer for 3 minutes. Add 125 ml (4 fl oz) of this to the chicken and ham, seasoning with pepper. Beat the meat and sauce together.

Fill the tubes with the mixture. Arrange them on top of the spinach, side by side in a single layer. Add two thirds of the Gruyère to the remaining sauce and heat gently, stirring, until the cheese has melted. Pour the sauce over the tubes, and sprinkle the remaining Gruyère on top. Bake in a preheated oven, 190°C, 375°F, Gas Mark 5 for 35 minutes or until golden. Serve hot, garnished with herb sprigs.

SERVES   6 as a main course

Nutritional content per serving: Carbohydrate: 37 g   Fat: 30 g   Fibre: 11 g   Kilocalories: 420

Cannelloni with Chicken and Ham

Rotolo

ROTOLO

THIS IS A KIND OF SAVOURY SWISS ROLL MADE FROM SPINACH, HAM, CHEESE AND PASTA

2 × 227 g (8 oz) packets frozen chopped
  spinach
250 g (8 oz) ricotta or curd cheese
50 g (2 oz) boiled ham, diced finely
50 g (2 oz) Parmesan cheese, freshly grated
grated nutmeg
1 egg, beaten
25 g (1 oz) butter, melted
salt and pepper
fig quarters to garnish
PASTA DOUGH:
125 g (4 oz) strong plain flour
pinch of salt
1 egg, beaten

Place the spinach in a pan, cover and cook until defrosted. Increase the heat and drive off any excess liquid. Transfer to a bowl and leave until cold. Meanwhile, make the pasta. Sift the flour and salt into a bowl, and mix in the egg. Turn the dough out on to a floured surface and knead with floured hands until smooth and shiny – about 10 minutes. Mix the ricotta into the spinach with the ham, half the Parmesan, the nutmeg and the egg. Season to taste.

Roll out the dough to a rectangle measuring about 35 × 30 cm (14 × 12 inches). Spread the spinach mixture over the pasta, leaving a 2.5 cm (1 inch) margin around the edges. Roll the dough into a Swiss roll shape, starting from one of the longest sides. Place the rotolo seam side down on a large piece of cheesecloth or muslin; roll up and tie the ends with string. Place the rotolo in a flameproof casserole. Cover with boiling salted water, half-cover with the lid and simmer for 45 minutes, turning the rotolo once during this time. Remove from the water and cool. When cold, unwrap and cut into 12 slices. Arrange in a buttered baking dish, overlapping slightly. Pour over the butter and sprinkle on the Parmesan. Bake in a preheated oven, 200°C, 400°F, Gas Mark 6, for 15 minutes or until golden. Garnish with fig quarters. Serve hot with a tomato sauce and salad.

SERVES 6 as a main course

Nutritional content per serving: Carbohydrate: 27 g   Fat: 22 g   Fibre: 8 g   Kilocalories: 405

STIR-FRIED CRAB WITH PORK AND NOODLES

THE CHINESE INFLUENCE IS CLEAR IN THIS SPICY-HOT MALAYSIAN RECIPE – IN THE METHOD OF STIR-FRYING, IN THE COMBINATION OF MEAT AND FISH TOGETHER IN ONE DISH, AND IN THE FLAVOURING INGREDIENTS SUCH AS SPRING ONIONS, GINGER, YELLOW BEAN SAUCE AND SOY SAUCE. IT SHOULD BE EATEN CHINESE-STYLE, WITH CHOPSTICKS. YOU CAN USE ALL WHITE CRAB MEAT OR A MIXTURE OF WHITE AND DARK, DEPENDING ON HOW MUCH YOU WANT TO SPEND

6 tablespoons sunflower oil

2 eggs

2 fresh red chillies, finely chopped

375 g (12 oz) crab meat

150 g (5 oz) medium or thread egg noodles

1 bunch spring onions, white and green
  parts separated and chopped

2.5 cm (1 inch) piece fresh root ginger,
  peeled and crushed

2 cloves garlic, crushed

3 tablespoons yellow bean sauce

375 g (12 oz) pork fillet, cut diagonally into
  3.5 × 1 cm (1½ × ½ inch) strips

200 g (7 oz) mangetout, topped and tailed

150 g (5 oz) fresh bean sprouts

1 red pepper, halved lengthways, cored,
  deseeded and cut into thin strips

150 ml (¼ pint) boiling stock (fish,
  vegetable or chicken)

4 tablespoons soy sauce

salt

Make the omelette to use as a garnish. Heat about 2 teaspoons of the oil in an omelette pan or small, heavy-based frying pan. Beat 1 egg in a bowl with half of the chopped chillies, about 2 tablespoons of the crab meat and a pinch of salt. When the oil is very hot, pour in the egg mixture and let it run to the sides of the pan, drawing the set mixture into the centre with a palette knife. Cook for a few minutes until the omelette is set, then slide it out on to a plate. Make another omelette in the same way, and leave them both to get cold.

Prepare the noodles. Bring a large saucepan of water to the boil. Add the noodles, cover the pan and immediately remove it from the heat. Leave to stand for 6 minutes, and drain well.

Heat 3 tablespoons of the oil in a wok or deep, heavy frying-pan, add the chopped white parts of the spring onions, the ginger, garlic and yellow bean sauce. Stir-fry over a gentle heat for 2-3 minutes to flavour the oil.

Increase the heat to moderate, add the strips of pork and stir-fry for 5 minutes until they are tender. Remove the spring onion mixture and the pork with a slotted spoon and set them aside on a plate.

Heat the remaining oil in the pan. Add the mangetout, bean sprouts and red pepper and stir-fry over a high heat for 2-3 minutes until they are tender but still crisp.

Return the pork and spring onion mixture to the pan and add the noodles. Pour in the stock or water and the soy sauce and stir-fry until the ingredients are evenly mixed and heated through. Gently fold in the remaining crab meat and heat it through. Taste the mixture and add salt, if necessary. Transfer to a warm serving platter.

Quickly roll up each omelette into a cigar shape, and cut them into thin strips. Sprinkle over the dish as a garnish, together with the reserved green parts of the spring onions. Serve at once. No accompaniment is necessary.

SERVES 4 as a main course

Nutritional content per serving:	Carbohydrate: 34 g	Fat: 40 g	Fibre: 5 g	Kilocalories: 700

Stir-Fried Crab with Pork and Noodles; Three-Cheese Lasagne

THREE-CHEESE LASAGNE

4 tablespoons olive oil

2 onions, chopped finely

825-900 g (1 lb 12 oz-2 lb) minced beef

2 large cloves garlic, crushed

2 × 397 g (14 oz) cans tomatoes, chopped with their juice

4 tablespoons tomato purée

150 ml (¼ pint) red wine

250 g (8 oz) mushrooms, chopped roughly

4 tablespoons chopped parsley

2 teaspoons chopped basil

2 bay leaves

2 teaspoons sugar

12 sheets 'no pre-cook' lasagne

500 g (1 lb) ricotta or curd cheese

375 g (12 oz) Mozzarella cheese, sliced thinly

125 g (4 oz) Parmesan cheese, freshly grated

salt and pepper

Heat the oil in a pan. Add the onions and cook, stirring frequently, until soft and golden. Add the beef and cook until the meat changes colour, stirring and pressing the meat to remove all lumps. Add the garlic, tomatoes, purée and wine and bring to the boil, stirring. Reduce the heat and add the mushrooms, herbs, bay leaves, sugar, salt and pepper. Cover and simmer gently for 3 hours, stirring occasionally.

When the sauce is cooked, remove the bay leaves. Pour half the sauce into a 5 cm (2 inch) deep baking dish measuring about 30 × 25 cm (12 × 10 inches). Cover with 6 sheets of lasagne. Dot half the ricotta on top, then half the Mozzarella and sprinkle on half the Parmesan. Repeat, ensuring the top layer of pasta is covered with cheese. Bake in a preheated oven 190°C, 375°F, Gas Mark 5, for 40-45 minutes.

Freezing: is recommended before baking. Cover the baking dish with foil and overwrap in a freezer bag. This will keep for up to 3 months. Bake from frozen, in a preheated oven, 190°C, 375°F, Gas Mark 5, still with the foil covering on, for about 1¼ hours, or until bubbling and completely heated through.

SERVES   6 as a main course

Nutritional content per serving: Carbohydrate: 37 g   Fat: 65 g   Fibre: 5 g   Kilocalories: 970

Ravioli with crab

THESE RAVIOLI ARE THE TRADITIONAL SQUARE SHAPE, BUT IF YOU PREFER TO MAKE THEM ROUND WITH FLUTED EDGES, FOLLOW THE INSTRUCTIONS IN THE RECIPE FOR PRAWN RAVIOLI IN FISH BROTH (SEE PAGE 12)

125 g (4 oz) crab meat, defrosted and
  thoroughly dried if frozen
3 tablespoons full-fat soft cream cheese
5 tablespoons finely chopped parsley
2 tablespoons finely snipped chives
salt and pepper
PASTA DOUGH:
200 g (7 oz) strong plain flour
¼ teaspoon salt
2 tablespoons finely chopped parsley
2 eggs, beaten
1 tablespoon olive oil, for cooking
SAUCE:
1 tablespoon butter
150 ml (¼ pint) soured cream
4 tablespoons milk
40 g (1½ oz) Parmesan cheese, freshly grated
1 tablespoon snipped chives
TO GARNISH:
parsley sprigs
grated Parmesan cheese

Mash the crab in a bowl with a fork. Add the cheese and herbs and season with salt and pepper to taste. Continue mashing until all the ingredients are evenly combined. Cover the bowl and set it aside.

Make the pasta dough. Sift the flour and salt into a bowl, stir in the parsley and mix in the eggs. Turn the dough out on to a floured surface and knead with floured hands until it is shiny and smooth – about 10 minutes.

Take one eighth of the dough and wrap the remainder in a damp tea towel. Roll out the unwrapped piece to a paper-thin strip measuring 35 × 7 cm (14 × 3 inches). Put 10 heaps of the filling mixture at regular intervals along one side of the strip of dough, each one about ¼ teaspoon. Fold the dough over the filling and press the edges together with a little water to seal them. Cut between each heap of filling to make ten 3.5 cm (1½ inch) square ravioli. Place on a floured tea towel. Repeat with the remaining dough and filling to make 80 ravioli altogether. Leave all the ravioli to dry for about 30 minutes, turning them over once.

Make the sauce. Melt the butter in a heavy saucepan. Add all the remaining ingredients with plenty of pepper and stir until heated through and the cheese is melted. Remove from the heat.

Bring a large saucepan of salted water to the boil and swirl in the oil. Add a batch of ravioli. Stir and bring back to the boil. Reduce the heat and boil, uncovered, for 4 minutes. Carefully remove the ravioli from the water with a slotted spoon, taking care not to break them. Keep them hot while cooking the remainder.

Quickly reheat the sauce without letting it boil. Put all the ravioli into a warm bowl, pour over the sauce and stir gently to mix the sauce and ravioli together. Divide equally between 4-6 warm soup plates. Garnish with parsley sprigs and grated Parmesan and serve at once. No accompaniment is necessary.

SERVES   4-6 as a starter

| Nutritional content per serving: | Carbohydrate: 41 g | Fat: 26 g | Fibre: 3 g | Kilocalories: 470 |

Ravioli with Crab; Tagliatelle with Fresh Salmon and Dill

TAGLIATELLE WITH FRESH SALMON AND DILL

300 g (10 oz) salmon fillet
3 tablespoons dry white wine
1 tablespoon chopped dill
25 g (1 oz) butter
425 g (14 oz) fresh tagliatelle verde
4 tablespoons double cream
salt and pepper
dill sprigs to garnish

Remove the skin and any bones from the salmon. Slice the flesh thinly and place it in a shallow dish with the wine and dill. Cover and leave for about 20 minutes to marinate, turning occasionally. Melt the butter in a heavy pan, add the salmon and marinade and season to taste. Poach gently for 8-10 minutes or until the fish is cooked.

Meanwhile, bring a large saucepan of salted water to the boil. Add the tagliatelle, stir and bring back to the boil. Reduce the heat and boil, uncovered for 3-4 minutes, or according to the packet instructions.

Drain the tagliatelle well. Add the cream to the salmon sauce and heat it through. Divide the tagliatelle equally between 4 warm soup plates. Pour over the sauce and garnish with dill sprigs. Serve at once.

SERVES   4 as a main course

Nutritional content per serving: Carbohydrate: 85 g   Fat: 20 g   Fibre: 3 g   Kilocalories: 630

Mongolian firepot

Have fun with your friends with this oriental version of a fondue party! Meat, fish and vegetables are cooked at the table in spicy, hot stock, then noodles are added and finally the stock is eaten as a soup. An oriental table setting is a must, with chopsticks, Chinese soup bowls and spoons, plus small bowls for the dipping sauce. Firepots can be obtained at oriental shops, but an ordinary fondue set can equally well be used

375 g (12 oz) fillet steak, trimmed of any fat
375 g (12 oz) boneless chicken breast, skinned
250 g (8 oz) peeled cooked prawns, defrosted and thoroughly dried if frozen
250 g (8 oz) firm tofu (bean curd), drained and cut into strips
250 g (8 oz) canned water chestnuts, drained
250 g (8 oz) small button mushrooms
2 peppers (1 red and 1 green), halved lengthways, cored, deseeded and cut into thin strips
250 g (8 oz) mangetout, topped and tailed
125 g (4 oz) fresh spinach leaves, stalks removed
75 g (3 oz) thread egg noodles

DIPPING SAUCE:
6 tablespoons smooth peanut butter
6 tablespoons soy sauce
2 tablespoons medium dry sherry
1-2 cloves garlic, according to taste, crushed
1-2 fresh red chillies, deseeded and chopped very finely, or ¼-½ teaspoon chilli powder, according to taste
red pepper slices to garnish

STOCK:
1.4 litres (3 pints) well-flavoured chicken stock, preferably homemade
3 spring onions, chopped finely
1 cm (½ inch) fresh root ginger, peeled and chopped finely
2 tablespoons medium dry sherry
2 tablespoons chopped coriander

Wrap the steak and chicken in foil and place them in the freezer for 30 minutes to 1 hour until they are half-frozen. Unwrap them and cut the meat across the grain into paper-thin strips with a very sharp knife.

Make the dipping sauce. Whisk all the ingredients together in a bowl. Divide the sauce equally between 4 individual dipping bowls.

Arrange equal amounts of steak, chicken, prawns, tofu, water chestnuts and vegetables on individual dinner plates. Make up each place setting at the table with dinner plate, chopsticks, bowl of dipping sauce, soup bowl and soup spoon.

Bring the stock to the boil on top of the stove. Add the spring onions, ginger, sherry and coriander. Carefully pour some of this boiling stock into the firepot or fondue pot and place it over a spirit burner in the centre of the table. Guests cook their own ingredients in the hot stock, using slotted spoons to lower them in and scoop them out, then chopsticks to dip the food into the sauce.

When the level of the stock in the pot is low, replenish it with more boiling stock from the stove. When all the ingredients are finished, pour any remaining stock from the firepot into the stock on the stove. Bring it back to the boil. Add the noodles, cover the pan tightly and immediately remove it from the heat. Leave to stand, tightly covered, for 6 minutes or according to the packet instructions. Ladle the soup into the soup bowls and serve at once. No accompaniment is necessary, although some guests may like extra soy sauce, for dipping and for adding to the noodle soup. Rice wine is the traditional drink with firepot, although dry white wine is equally suitable.

SERVES 4

Nutritional content per serving: Carbohydrate: 31 g   Fat: 30 g   Fibre: 7 g   Kilocalories: 710

Mongolian Firepot; Mee Krob

MEE KROB

MEE KROB IS A THAI SPECIALITY, MADE WITH RICE VERMICELLI. THIS RECIPE USES THREAD EGG NOODLES, WHICH ARE EASIER TO OBTAIN

250 g (8 oz) thread egg noodles

3 tablespoons groundnut or corn oil

1 large onion, chopped finely

2 cloves garlic, crushed

175 g (6 oz) boneless chicken breast, skinned and sliced thinly across the grain

175 g (6 oz) pork fillet, sliced thinly across the grain

125 g (4 oz) green beans, topped and tailed and sliced in half diagonally

125 g (4 oz) peeled cooked prawns, defrosted and thoroughly dried if frozen

300 g (10 oz) tofu (bean curd), drained and cubed (optional)

3-4 tablespoons cider or wine vinegar

3-4 tablespoons caster sugar

soy sauce or anchovy essence, to taste

oil for deep-frying

½ teaspoon chilli powder

bean sprouts to garnish

Bring a large saucepan of water to the boil. Add the noodles, cover the pan and immediately remove it from the heat. Leave to stand for 6 minutes. Drain and dry the noodles thoroughly. Heat the oil in a wok or deep, heavy frying-pan. Add the onion and stir-fry over a gentle heat for about 5 minutes until it is tender. Increase the heat and add the garlic, chicken, pork and green beans and stir-fry for 3-4 minutes. Add the prawns and tofu, if using, and stir-fry for a further 2-3 minutes.

Gradually stir in the vinegar, sugar, soy sauce or anchovy essence to taste – the sauce should be both sweet and salty in flavour. Remove the pan from the heat. Turn the mixture into a bowl and set it aside.

Heat the oil for deep-frying until hot but not smoking. Add one quarter of the noodles and fry until crisp and lightly brown. Remove and drain on kitchen paper while frying the rest.

Set one quarter of the fried noodles aside for the garnish. Return about half the mee krob mixture to the wok, add half of the remaining noodles and half of the chilli powder and toss gently to combine the ingredients and heat them through, taking care not to break the noodles. Transfer to a warm serving platter, cover and keep hot while frying the remaining mee krob, noodles and chilli powder in the same way. When the platter is full, garnish with bean sprouts. Serve at once.

SERVES   6 as a main course

Nutritional content per serving: Carbohydrate: 42 g   Fat: 16 g   Fibre: 3 g   Kilocalories: 420

Seafood lasagne

Rich and creamy, this lasagne is made with layers of monkfish and shellfish in a white sauce, pasta and tomato sauce. It makes a deliciously different change from the usual meat lasagne

2 tablespoons olive oil

1 × 250 g (8.82 oz) packet lasagne verde

15 g (½ oz) butter

500 g (1 lb) monkfish fillet, skinned and cut into cubes

500 g (1 lb) prepared mixed shellfish (prawns, crab or crab sticks, lobster, scallops), defrosted and thoroughly dried if frozen

65 g (2½ oz) Cheddar cheese, grated

40 g (1½ oz) Parmesan cheese, freshly grated

SAUCE:

2 tablespoons olive oil

1 onion, chopped finely

1 large clove garlic, crushed

1 × 397 g (14 oz) can tomatoes, chopped with their juice

2 tablespoons tomato purée

150 ml (¼ pint) dry white wine

2 teasoons chopped oregano

2 teaspoons chopped basil

salt and pepper

WHITE SAUCE:

50 g (2 oz) butter

50 g (2 oz) plain flour

450 ml (¾ pint) milk

pinch of ground mace

150 ml (¼ pint) double cream

salt and pepper

Make the tomato sauce first. Heat the oil in a heavy saucepan. Add the onion and cook gently, stirring frequently, until it has softened – about 5 minutes. Add the garlic, tomatoes, tomato purée and wine and bring to the boil. Reduce the heat, add the herbs and season with salt and pepper to taste. Cover the pan and simmer gently for 30 minutes, stirring occasionally.

Meanwhile, make the white sauce. Melt the butter in a heavy pan, add the flour and cook, stirring, for 1 minute. Gradually blend in the milk, bring to the boil, still stirring, and simmer for 3 minutes. Add the mace and season with salt and pepper to taste. Remove the pan from the heat and stir in the cream.

Bring a large saucepan of salted water to the boil, swirl in 1 tablespoon of the oil and add 4 sheets of lasagne. Bring back to the boil. Reduce the heat and boil, uncovered, for 6-8 minutes, or according to the packet instructions. Remove and place in a single layer on a clean tea towel. Repeat with the remaining lasagne.

Melt the butter and the remaining oil in a large frying pan. Add the monkfish and fry, turning it over until it is lightly coloured. Remove with a slotted spoon and set aside. Add the shellfish to the pan and stir-fry until lightly coloured. Remove with a slotted spoon and set aside with the monkfish. Add the monkfish and shellfish to the white sauce. Adjust the seasoning if necessary. Pour one third of this sauce into the bottom of a 5 cm (2 inch) deep baking dish measuring about 30 × 20 cm (12 × 8 inches). Cover with 4 sheets of lasagne, then half the tomato sauce. Repeat with 4 more sheets of lasagne, then with one third of the fish sauce, 4 more sheets of lasagne and the remaining tomato sauce. Finish with the remaining fish sauce and cover thickly with the grated cheeses. Bake in a preheated oven 190°C, 375°F, Gas Mark 5, for about 30 minutes or until golden brown and bubbling. Serve as a main course with a tossed green salad.

Freezing: is recommended before baking. Cover the baking dish with foil and overwrap in a freezer bag. This will keep for up to 1 month. Bake from frozen in a preheated oven, 190°C, 375°F, Gas Mark 5, still with the foil covering on, for about 45 minutes or until bubbling and completely heated through.

SERVES 4-6

Nutritional content per serving: Carbohydrate: 73 g   Fat: 67 g   Fibre: 4 g   Kilocalories:1150

Seafood Lasagne; Spaghetti with Shellfish

SPAGHETTI WITH SHELLFISH

3 tablespoons olive oil

2 cloves garlic, crushed

1 × 50 g (2 oz) can anchovies in oil, drained and dried

3 tablespoons chopped parsley

1 tablespoon chopped dill

1 red pepper, halved lengthways, cored, deseeded and sliced thinly

125 g (4 oz) prepared squid, cut into rings

150 ml (¼ pint) dry white wine

2 pinches of crushed dried chillies

1 large pinch saffron threads

175 g (6 oz) shelled cooked mussels

175 g (6 oz) peeled cooked prawns, defrosted and thoroughly dried if frozen

150 ml (¼ pint) fish stock

4 shelled scallops, diced (including the coral)

375-425 g (12-14 oz) spaghetti

pepper

TO GARNISH:

Mediterranean prawns

mussel shells

Heat 2 tablespoons of the oil in a heavy pan. Add the garlic and cook until golden. Add the anchovies and herbs and stir, pressing the anchovies so that they break and become almost puréed. Add the pepper and squid and cook gently for 5 minutes, stirring. Add the wine, chillies, saffron and pepper, increase the heat and simmer for 10 minutes until reduced to a thick sauce. Add the mussels, prawns and stock and simmer for 10 minutes until slightly reduced. Stir in scallops, cover and cook for 5 minutes. Remove from the heat.

Bring a pan of water to the boil. Add the pasta, stir and bring back to the boil. Reduce the heat and boil, for 10-12 minutes, or according to packet instructions, stirring occasionally. Drain the pasta. Reheat the sauce gently. Transfer the pasta to a warm bowl, add the remaining oil and toss. Divide the pasta between 4 plates, pour on the sauce and serve. Garnish with prawns and mussel shells.

Freezing: is recommended for the sauce. Freeze in a rigid, airtight container. This will keep for up to 1 month. Defrost overnight in a refrigerator or at room temperature for 4-6 hours. Reheat gently, for at least 10 minutes. Continue as above.

SERVES 4

Nutritional content per serving: Carbohydrate: 75 g   Fat: 17 g   Fibre: 4 g   Kilocalories: 610

SALADS

SHARP AND SPICY, SWEET AND SUBTLE, THE COMBINATION OF FLAVOURS IN PASTA SALADS CAN BE AS SIMPLE OR VARIED AS YOU WISH. ENHANCED WITH DELICIOUS DRESSINGS THESE SUMPTUOUS SALADS WILL ADD A COMPLETELY NEW DIMENSION TO YOUR SUMMER COOKING.

PASTA FISH SALAD

200 g (7 oz) dried pasta shells
175 g (6 oz) peeled cooked prawns, defrosted
  and thoroughly dried if frozen
1 × 198 g (7 oz) can tuna, drained and
  flaked
1 × 250 g (8 oz) can mussels in brine,
  drained and chopped roughly
6 spring onions, chopped finely
2 firm, ripe tomatoes, skinned and diced
salt and pepper
spring onions to garnish
MAYONNAISE:
1 egg yolk
150 ml (¼ pint) groundnut or corn oil
1 teaspoon tomato purée
1 tablespoon white wine vinegar

Bring a large saucepan of salted water to the boil. Add the pasta, stir and bring back to the boil. Reduce the heat and boil, uncovered, for 10 minutes or according to the packet instructions, stirring occasionally.

Drain the pasta, refresh it briefly under cold water to prevent overcooking, drain again well and leave to cool. Make the mayonnaise. Put the egg yolk in a bowl with salt and pepper to taste and beat it well. Beat in the oil a drop at a time until the mixture emulsifies, then add the oil more quickly, in a thin, steady stream. Whisk in the tomato purée. Thin down the mixture with the wine vinegar. Cover the bowl and set it aside. When the pasta is cold, turn it into a large bowl and add the prawns, tuna, mussels, spring onions and tomatoes. Season with salt and pepper to taste. Fold the ingredients gently together. Carefully fold in the mayonnaise. Cover the bowl tightly and place it in the refrigerator to chill for 1-2 hours. Let the salad come to room temperature before serving, then transfer to a bowl. Serve as a main course salad with extra mayonnaise, if desired. Garnish with spring onions.

SERVES 4-6

Nutritional content per serving: Carbohydrate: 44 g   Fat: 50 g   Fibre: 3 g   Kilocalories: 765

PASTA SALAD NIÇOISE

250 g (8 oz) dried farfalle (pasta bows)
250 g (8 oz) green beans, topped and tailed
2 firm ripe tomatoes, skinned and cut into
  thin wedges
1 × 198 g (7 oz) can tuna, drained and
  flaked
2 tablespoons chopped mixed herbs
  (tarragon, basil, parsley)
2 hard-boiled eggs, shelled and quartered
1 × 50 g (2 oz) can anchovies in oil,
  drained and soaked in milk for 20 minutes
50 g (2 oz) black olives, pitted
salt and pepper
DRESSING:
6 tablespoons olive oil
3 tablespoons tarragon vinegar
½ teaspoon mustard powder
pinch of sugar

Bring a large saucepan of salted water to the boil. Add the farfalle, stir and bring back to the boil. Reduce the heat and boil, uncovered, for 10 minutes or according to packet instructions, stirring occasionally.

Cook the beans in a little lightly salted boiling water for 3-4 minutes until just tender but still with a crunchy bite. Drain, refresh them briefly under cold running water and drain well again.

Whisk the dressing ingredients together in the bottom of a large bowl. Drain the farfalle and refresh it briefly under cold running water to prevent overcooking. Drain well again and transfer to the bowl and stir in the beans. Toss the beans and pasta well to mix them with the dressing. Season to taste. Leave to cool, stirring occasionally.

When the pasta is cold, add the tomatoes, tuna and herbs. Season with pepper to taste and fold all the ingredients gently together. Transfer the salad to a serving platter and arrange the eggs around the edge. Drain and dry the anchovies, cut them in half lengthways, and arrange them on top of the salad with the olives. Serve at once.

SERVES 4-6

Nutritional content per serving: Carbohydrate: 56 g   Fat: 37 g   Fibre: 5 g   Kilocalories: 640

Pasta Fish Salad; Pasta Salad Niçoise

Salami salad

250 g (8 oz) fresh paglia e fieno
4 tablespoons olive oil
1 tablespoon white wine vinegar
125 g (4 oz) thinly sliced Italian salami,
  skinned and cut into bite size pieces
1 small fennel bulb, sliced
2 peppers (1 red and 1 green), halved
  lengthways, cored, deseeded and cut into
  thin strips
1 red onion, chopped
12 black olives, pitted and sliced into rings
salt and pepper
dill sprigs to garnish

Bring a large saucepan of salted water to the boil. Add the pasta, stir and bring back to the boil. Reduce the heat and boil, uncovered, for 3-4 minutes or according to packet instructions, stirring occasionally.

Meanwhile, whisk the oil and vinegar together in the bottom of a large bowl. Drain the pasta and refresh it briefly under cold running water to prevent overcooking. Drain it again well, and cut into short lengths. Place the pasta in the bowl and toss it well to mix it with the dressing. Season to taste. Leave to cool, stirring occasionally.

When the pasta is cold, add the salami, fennel, peppers, onion and olives. Fold the ingredients together gently. Cover the bowl tightly and chill in the refrigerator for about 30 minutes. Before serving toss the salad and garnish with dill sprigs.

SERVES 4

Nutritional content per serving: Carbohydrate: 18 g   Fat: 32 g   Fibre: 2 g   Kilocalories: 380

Coronation salad

IF YOU ARE WORRIED ABOUT THE MAYONNAISE CURDLING, PUT 1 TABLESPOON READY-MADE MAYONNAISE IN THE BOWL WITH THE EGG YOLK AND SPICES BEFORE STARTING TO BEAT IN THE OIL.

250 g (8 oz) dried rigatoni or penne (quills)
1 tablespoon olive oil
500 g (1 lb) boneless turkey breast, skinned
  and sliced into bite-sized pieces
1 red pepper, halved lengthways, cored,
  deseeded and cut into thin strips
1 green pepper, halved lengthways, cored,
  deseeded and cut into thin strips
2 tablespoons mango chutney or apricot jam
salt and pepper
MAYONNAISE:
1 egg yolk
1 teaspoon curry powder
1-2 teaspoons paprika, according to taste
¼ teaspoon chilli powder, or to taste
150 ml (¼ pint) groundnut or corn oil
1 tablespoon lemon juice, or to taste

Bring a large saucepan of salted water to the boil. Add the pasta, stir and bring back to the boil. Reduce the heat and boil, uncovered, for 13 minutes or according to the packet instructions, stirring occasionally.

Drain the pasta and refresh it briefly under cold running water to prevent overcooking. Drain it again well and cut each piece in half with kitchen scissors to make short lengths. Leave them to cool.

Meanwhile, make the mayonnaise. Put the egg yolk, curry powder, paprika and chilli powder in a bowl and season to taste. Beat well to mix the ingredients. Beat in the oil a drop at a time until the mixture emulsifies, then add the oil more quickly, in a thin, steady stream. Thin down the mayonnaise with lemon juice to taste. Cover the bowl and set aside. Heat the oil in a frying pan, add the turkey and stir-fry over a moderate heat for 10 minutes. Add the pepper and stir-fry for a further 5-10 minutes or until the turkey is tender. Remove the turkey and peppers. Leave to drain and cool on kitchen paper.

If there are any pieces of fruit in the chutney or jam, chop them finely before stirring them into the mayonnaise. Mix together the pasta, turkey and peppers in a large bowl and carefully fold in the mayonnaise. Cover the bowl tightly and place it in the refrigerator for 1-2 hours. Let the salad come to room temperature before serving.

SERVES 4-6

Nutritional content per serving: Carbohydrate: 58 g   Fat: 46 g   Fibre: 3 g   Kilocalories: 790

SAUSAGE, BEAN AND PASTA SALAD

200 g (7 oz) dried pasta shells

150 g (5 oz) frozen petits pois

1 × 532 g (15.25 oz) can red kidney beans, drained and rinsed

1 × 415 g (13.6 oz) can flageolet beans, drained and rinsed

1 × 340 g (12 oz) can sweetcorn and peppers, drained

175 g (6 oz) garlic sausage, skinned and chopped into bite-sized pieces

½ onion, chopped finely

3 firm ripe tomatoes, skinned and diced

salt and pepper

mint sprigs to garnish

DRESSING:

4 tablespoons chopped mint

2 cloves garlic, crushed

3 tablespoons olive oil

1 tablespoon white wine vinegar

Bring a large saucepan of salted water to the boil. Add the pasta shells, stir and bring back to the boil. Reduce the heat and boil, uncovered, for 10 minutes or according to packet instructions, stirring occasionally.

Meanwhile, cook the petits pois in a little salted boiling water for 3-4 minutes or according to the packet instructions. Drain well.

Whisk the dressing ingredients together in the bottom of a large bowl. Drain the pasta shells and refresh them briefly under cold running water. Drain them again well. Place the pasta in the bowl and stir in the petits pois. Toss well to mix the pasta and petits pois with the dressing. Season to taste. Leave to cool, stirring occasionally.

When the pasta is cold, add both kinds of beans, the sweetcorn and peppers, garlic sausage, onion and tomatoes. Season with salt and pepper to taste. Fold the ingredients together gently. Cover the bowl tightly and place it in the refrigerator to chill for 1-2 hours.

To serve, toss the salad again to mix the ingredients evenly and let it come to room temperature. Adjust the seasoning if necessary. Transfer to a serving bowl and garnish with sprigs of mint.

SERVES 4-6

Nutritional content per serving: Carbohydrate: 88 g   Fat: 33 g   Fibre: 24 g   Kilocalories: 750

Salami Salad; Coronation Salad; Sausage, Bean and Pasta Salad

BROCCOLI, PASTA AND PRAWN SALAD

250 g (8 oz) dried pasta shells
250 g (8 oz) broccoli florets, stalks removed,
   divided into tiny sprigs
250 g (8 oz) peeled cooked prawns, defrosted
   and thoroughly dried if frozen
salt and pepper
lime slices to garnish
MAYONNAISE:
1 egg yolk
finely grated rind and juice of 1 lime
125 ml (4 fl oz) groundnut or corn oil
50 ml (2 fl oz) olive oil

Bring a large saucepan of salted water to the boil. Add the pasta shells, stir and bring back to the boil. Reduce the heat and boil, uncovered, for 10 minutes or according to packet instructions, stirring occasionally.

Cook the broccoli in a little lightly salted boiling water for 2-3 minutes until it is tender but still with a crunchy bite. Drain and refresh under cold running water. Drain again well and leave to cool.

Drain the pasta shells and refresh briefly under cold running water to prevent overcooking. Drain them again well and leave to cool.

Meanwhile, make the mayonnaise. Place the egg yolk in a bowl with the lime rind and season with salt and pepper to taste. Beat the egg well and beat in the groundnut oil a drop at a time until the mixture emulsifies. Add the oil more quickly, in a thin, stready stream. Add the olive oil in the same way, then thin down the mayonnaise with the lime juice.

Put the pasta, broccoli and prawns in a large bowl and toss them together well. Add the mayonnaise and season with salt and pepper to taste. Toss the ingredients again until they are evenly coated. Cover the bowl tightly and place it in the refrigerator for 1-2 hours to chill.

To serve, toss the salad again to mix the ingredients evenly and let it come to room temperature. Adjust the seasoning, if necessary. Divide equally between 4-6 individual plates or dishes and garnish with lime slices. Serve for a starter with extra mayonnaise if desired.

SERVES 4-6

Nutritional content per serving:	Carbohydrate: 54 g	Fat: 41 g	Fibre: 4 g	Kilocalories: 675

Broccoli, Pasta and Prawn Salad

Oriental Crab and Pasta Salad

ORIENTAL CRAB AND PASTA SALAD

175 g (6 oz) dried egg vermicelli

4 tablespoons groundnut or corn oil

2 large cloves garlic, crushed

1-2 fresh red chillies, according to taste
deseeded and chopped finely

6 spring onions, chopped finely

50 g (2 oz) dark crab meat or crab pâté

4 tablespoons soy sauce

2 tablespoons lime or lemon juice, or to taste

250 g (8 oz) white crab meat, flaked

¼ large cucumber, skinned and cut into
matchstick strips

lettuce leaves, shredded

salt and pepper

parsley sprigs to garnish

Bring a large saucepan of salted water to the boil. Add the vermicelli, stir and bring back to the boil. Reduce the heat and boil, uncovered, for 5 minutes or according to the packet instructions, stirring occasionally.

Drain the vermicelli and rinse it briefly under cold running water to prevent overcooking. Drain it again well and leave to cool.

Heat 1 tablespoon of the oil in a small, frying-pan. Add the garlic, chillies and half the spring onions and stir fry for 1-2 minutes until the mixture gives off a spicy aroma. Transfer to a bowl and leave to cool.

Put the dark crab meat or pâté in the bottom of a large bowl. Add the garlic, chilli and spring onion mixture, the remaining oil, the soy sauce and 2 tablespoons lime or lemon juice. Whisk vigorously to make a smooth dressing. When the pasta is cold, add it to the bowl of dressing and stir well until the strands of vermicelli are evenly coated. Add the flaked white crab meat, the remaining spring onions and the cucumber and fold them together gently. Add salt and pepper to taste, and more lime or lemon juice if liked. Cover the bowl tightly and place in the refrigerator to chill for 30 minutes to 1 hour.

To serve, line 6 individual plates with shredded lettuce leaves. Divide the salad between them and garnish with sprigs of parsley.

SERVES   6 as a starter

Nutritional content per serving: Carbohydrate: 23 g   Fat: 15 g   Fibre: 2 g   Kilocalories: 280

INSALATA DI MARE

500 g (1 lb) prepared squid, cut into rings
400 ml (14 fl oz) Italian dry red wine
4 cloves garlic, crushed
500 g (1 lb) fresh mussels, soaked in cold
  water for 1 hour
1 bouquet garni (parsley, thyme and bay
  leaf)
250 g (8 oz) dried farfalle (pasta bows)
9 tablespoons Italian extra-virgin olive oil
juice of 1 lemon
250 g (8 oz) peeled cooked prawns, defrosted
  and thoroughly dried if frozen
1 × 50 g (2 oz) can anchovies in oil,
  drained and soaked in milk for 20 minutes
2 × 185 g (6½ oz) cans pimientos (sweet
  red peppers), drained and sliced thinly
4 teaspoons chopped basil
salt and pepper
basil sprigs to garnish

Place the squid rings in an earthenware casserole or baking dish. Pour over 300 ml (½ pint) of the wine and stir in half the crushed garlic. Cover and cook in a preheated oven, 180°C, 350°F, Gas Mark 4 for about 1½ hours or until the squid is tender, stirring occasionally.

Drain the mussels. Discard any that are open and do not close when tapped sharply on the work surface. Scrub the closed mussels under cold running water and remove the beards. Put the mussels in a heavy pan, pour in the remaining wine and add the bouquet garni. Bring to the boil, cover the pan tightly and cook over a high heat for 6-8 minutes. Shake the pan vigorously from time to time, until all the mussels have opened. Drain, then leave them until they are cool enough to handle, then remove the meat. Reserve a few whole ones for the garnish. Discard any that have not opened.

Bring a large saucepan of salted water to the boil. Add the farfalle, stir and bring back to the boil. Reduce the heat and boil, uncovered, for 10 minutes or according to packet instructions, stirring occasionally.

Whisk the olive oil, lemon juice and remaining garlic together in a large bowl. Drain the farfalle and refresh them briefly under cold running water to prevent overcooking. Drain them again and transfer to the bowl. Stir in the shelled mussels and the prawns. Toss well to mix. Season with salt and pepper to taste.

When the squid is tender, drain it thoroughly and rinse briefly under cold running water. Add it to the salad. Drain the anchovies, pat them dry on kitchen paper and cut them in half with kitchen scissors. Add them to the salad with the pimientos, and basil. Toss all the ingredients together well. Leave the salad to cool, stirring occasionally.

Cover the bowl tightly and chill in the refrigerator for about 30 minutes. Before serving, toss the salad again. Transfer to a bowl. Garnish with the reserved mussels and basil and serve chilled.

Microwave: Place the squid in a dish with only 4 tablespoons of the wine and half the garlic. Cover and cook on High Power for 3-4 minutes, stirring once, until tender. Leave to cool. Prepare the mussels as above then place in a bowl with 3 fl oz (75 ml) wine and the bouquet garni. Cover and cook on High Power for 5 minutes, shaking the dish twice. Drain and prepare as above. Place the pasta in a bowl with 1.2 litres (2 pints) boiling salted water and cook for 10-12 minutes, stirring once. Leave to stand for 3 minutes then drain. Make the dressing, adding the pasta, mussels, prawns, squid, anchovies, pimientos and basil as above. Garnish and serve.

SERVES 6

Nutritional content per serving:	Carbohydrate: 38 g	Fat: 26 g	Fibre: 2 g	Kilocalories: 560

Insalata Di Mare; Roman Salad

ROMAN SALAD

250 g (8 oz) fresh tagliatelle verde

4 tablespoons Italian extra-virgin olive oil

1 tablespoon white wine vinegar

4 spring onions, chopped finely

4 small, firm ripe tomatoes, skinned and diced

1 × 198 g (7 oz) can tuna, drained and flaked

1 × 50 g (2 oz) can anchovies in oil, drained and chopped roughly

25 g (1 oz) parsley, chopped finely

4 hard-boiled eggs, shelled

salt and pepper

Bring a large saucepan of salted water to the boil. Add the tagliatelle, stir and bring back to the boil. Reduce the heat and boil, uncovered, for 2-3 minutes or according to the packet instructions, stirring occasionally. Meanwhile, whisk the oil and vinegar together in the bottom of a large bowl.

Drain the tagliatelle and refresh it briefly under cold running water to prevent overcooking. Drain it again well and transfer it to the bowl. Toss the pasta with the dressing and season with salt and pepper to taste. Leave to cool, stirring occasionally.

When the pasta is cold, add the onions, tomatoes, tuna, anchovies and parsley. Halve the eggs. Remove the yolks and set them aside. Chop the whites finely and add them to the salad. Fold the salad ingredients together gently. Cover the bowl tightly and place it in the refrigerator to chill for 1-2 hours to allow the flavours to mature and mingle. Sieve the reserved egg yolks.

Before serving, fold the salad ingredients together again. Adjust the seasoning if necessary and transfer to a serving bowl. Sprinkle the sieved egg yolks on top and serve chilled. Serve as a starter, or as a salad to accompany meat or poultry.

SERVES 4-6

Nutritional content per serving: Carbohydrate: 54 g   Fat: 33 g   Fibre: 3 g   Kilocalories: 615

INSALATA DELICATA

THIS 'DELICATE' SALAD IS ABSOLUTELY DELICIOUS – CREAMY IN TEXTURE AND SUBTLE IN FLAVOUR, WITH A HINT OF FRESH TARRAGON

200 g (7 oz) dried pasta shells

250 g (8 oz) cooked chicken breast, skinned and cut into thin slivers

125 g (4 oz) peeled cooked prawns, defrosted and thoroughly dried if frozen

1 ripe avocado

salt and pepper

lettuce leaves to serve

tarragon sprigs to garnish

MAYONNAISE:

1 egg yolk

½ teaspoon Dijon mustard

150 ml (¼ pint) groundnut or corn oil

2 teaspoons tarragon vinegar

2 teaspoons chopped tarragon

Bring a large saucepan of salted water to the boil. Add the pasta shells, stir and bring back to the boil. Reduce the heat and boil, uncovered, for 10 minutes or according to the packet instructions, stirring occasionally.

Drain the pasta and refresh it briefly under cold running water to prevent overcooking. Drain it again well and leave to cool.

Meanwhile, make the mayonnaise. Beat the egg yolk and mustard together in a bowl, seasoned with salt and pepper to taste. Beat in the oil a drop at a time until the mixture emulsifies, then add the oil more quickly, in a thin, steady stream. Thin down the mayonnaise with the tarragon vinegar. Add the tarragon, cover the bowl and set it aside.

Mix the pasta, chicken and prawns together in a bowl. Halve the avocado lengthways and remove the stone and skin. Slice the flesh thinly and gently fold it into the salad. Cover the bowl tightly and chill in the refrigerator for 30 minutes.

To serve the salad, line a serving dish with lettuce leaves. Place the salad into the dish and spoon over the mayonnaise. Garnish with sprigs of tarragon.

SERVES 4

Nutritional content per serving: Carbohydrate: 43 g   Fat: 41 g   Fibre: 2 g   Kilocalories: 750

Insalata Delicata

Courgette and Pasta Salad

COURGETTE AND PASTA SALAD

250 g (8 oz) dried farfalle (pasta bows)
375 g (12 oz) small courgettes, sliced thinly
125 g (4 oz) blue-veined cheese
   (eg Gorgonzola, Danish blue, blue Brie) at
   room temperature
2 tablespoons groundnut oil
1 tablespoon red wine vinegar
3 firm ripe tomatoes, skinned and cut into
   wedges
50 g (2 oz) black olives, pitted
1 tablespoon chopped basil
salt and pepper
basil sprigs to garnish

Bring a pan of salted water to the boil. Add the farfalle, stir and bring back to the boil. Place the courgettes in a colander. Cover and place over the pan of pasta. Reduce the heat and boil for 10 minutes or according to packet instructions, stirring occasionally. Remove the cheese rind. Put half the cheese in a bowl and mash it with a fork. Gradually work in the oil, then the vinegar, until smooth.

Remove the colander of courgettes from the pan and set it aside. Drain the pasta and refresh briefly under cold running water. Drain again well and transfer to the bowl of dressing. Add the courgettes. Toss well to mix. Leave to cool, stirring occasionally.

When the pasta is cold, crumble the remaining cheese and add it to the pasta with the tomatoes, olives and basil. Season to taste. Fold the ingredients together. Cover the bowl and chill for about 30 minutes. Before serving toss again. Garnish with basil.

Microwave: Place the pasta in a bowl with 1.2 litres (2 pints) boiling salted water and cook on High Power for 10-12 minutes, stirring once. Cover and leave to stand while cooking the courgettes. Place the courgettes in a bowl with a knob of butter, cover and cook on High for 4-5 minutes. Drain the pasta and courgettes. Prepare as above.

SERVES 4-6

Nutritional content per serving: Carbohydrate: 57 g   Fat: 21 g   Fibre: 3 g   Kilocalories: 480

CHARGRILLED PEPPER SALAD

IT IS ESSENTIAL TO WRAP THE PEPPERS *IMMEDIATELY* AFTER CHARGRILLING SO THAT THE FLAVOUR IS CONCENTRATED

3 peppers (1 red, 1 green, 1 yellow)
250 g (8 oz) dried pasta twists
8 tablespoons hazelnut, walnut or olive oil
2 tablespoons raspberry or red wine vinegar
2 teaspoons mustard with herbs
1 × 300 g (10.6 oz) can whole button
  mushrooms, drained
1 × 50 g (2 oz) can anchovies in oil, drained
  and chopped roughly
salt and pepper
basil leaves to garnish

Pierce the peppers one at a time in the stalk end with a fork and hold over the flame of a gas hob. Rotate the peppers until they are charred black on all sides. Wrap them immediately in several thicknesses of kitchen paper and overwrap in 2-3 tea towels to retain the heat. Leave overnight. The next day, bring a large saucepan of salted water to the boil, add the pasta twists, stir and bring back to the boil. Reduce the heat and boil, uncovered, for 10 minutes or according to the packet instructions, stirring occasionally.

Whisk the oil, vinegar and mustard together in the bottom of a large bowl. Drain the pasta and refresh it briefly under cold water. Drain it again and place it in the bowl. Toss the pasta well to mix it with the dressing. Season to taste. Leave to cool, stirring occasionally.

Meanwhile, unwrap the peppers and hold them one at a time under cold running water. Rub off the charred skins with your fingers. Open up the peppers and remove the cores and seeds. Drain and dry them on kitchen paper and cut them lengthways into thin strips.

Combine the pepper strips and the cold pasta with the mushrooms and anchovies, tossing them together. Cover the bowl tightly and place in the refrigerator for 1-2 hours. Before serving, toss the salad. Garnish with basil.

SERVES 6

Nutritional content per serving: Carbohydrate: 36 g   Fat: 22 g   Fibre: 3 g   Kilocalories: 370

GERMAN NOODLE SALAD

250 g (8 oz) dried macaroni or pasta shells
1 × 535 g (19.0 oz) can frankfurters in brine,
  drained and chopped into bite-sized pieces
1 × 283 g (10 oz) can garden peas, drained
5 pickled gherkins, drained and chopped
2 hard-boiled eggs, shelled and chopped
½ onion, chopped finely
4 tablespoons mayonnaise
2 tablespoons wine vinegar
1 teaspoon German mustard
salt and pepper
TO GARNISH:
chervil sprigs
hard-boiled egg wedges (optional)

Bring a large saucepan of salted water to the boil. Add the pasta, stir and bring back to the boil. Reduce the heat and boil, uncovered, for 10 minutes or according to the packet instructions, stirring occasionally.

Drain the pasta and refresh it briefly under cold running water to prevent overcooking. Drain it again well and leave to cool.

When the pasta is cold, transfer it to a large bowl and stir in the remaining ingredients, tossing them together. Season with salt and pepper to taste. Cover the bowl tightly and place it in the refrigerator for 1-2 hours to chill. Turn into a serving bowl and serve chilled. Garnish with sprigs of chervil and hard-boiled egg wedges, if desired.

SERVES 4-6

Nutritional content per serving: Carbohydrate: 60 g   Fat: 47 g   Fibre: 11 g   Kilocalories: 755

Chargrilled Pepper Salad; German Noodle Salad; Pasta Salad with Tuna and Beans

PASTA SALAD WITH TUNA AND BEANS

250 g (8 oz) dried wholewheat pasta shells

1 × 440 g (15½ oz) can red kidney beans, drained and rinsed

1 × 270 g (8½ oz) can borlotti or flageolet beans, drained and rinsed

1 × 50 g (2 oz) can anchovies, drained and soaked in milk for 20 minutes

1 × 198 g (7 oz) can tuna, drained and flaked

1 small, red onion, sliced thinly into rings

salt and pepper

DRESSING:

6 tablespoons olive oil

3 tablespoons lemon juice

2 tablespoons finely chopped parsley

Bring a large saucepan of salted water to the boil. Add the pasta, stir and bring back to the boil. Reduce the heat and boil, uncovered, for 10-12 minutes or according to packet instructions, stirring occasionally.

Whisk the dressing ingredients together in the bottom of a large bowl. Drain the pasta, refresh it briefly under cold running water to prevent it overcooking and drain again well. Turn the pasta into the bowl and stir in the beans. Toss them well to mix them with the dressing. Season with the salt and pepper to taste. Leave to cool, stirring occasionally. Meanwhile, drain and dry the anchovies and chop them roughly.

When the pasta is cold, add the anchovies, tuna and onion and toss them well to combine with the other ingredients. Cover the bowl tightly and place in the refrigerator to chill for about 30 minutes. Toss again before serving, adjust the seasoning if necessary and transfer to a serving bowl. Serve chilled with warm wholemeal pitta bread.

SERVES 4-6

Nutritional content per serving: Carbohydrate: 61 g   Fat: 35 g   Fibre: 15 g   Kilocalories: 625

QUICK AND EASY

THERE'S NOTHING SO CONVENIENT AS PASTA. PUT TOGETHER WITH JUST A FEW INGREDIENTS FROM YOUR STORE CUPBOARD, IT CAN BE MADE INTO SUBSTANTIAL MEALS IN MINUTES. ALL THE RECIPES IN THIS CHAPTER CAN BE MADE IN AROUND HALF AN HOUR.

TAGLIATELLE WITH ASPARAGUS AND CREAM

1 × 411 g (14.5 oz) can asparagus cuts and
    tips, drained
25 g (1 oz) butter
2 tablespoons plain flour
175 ml (6 fl oz) hot milk
150 ml (¼ pint) single cream
2 tablespoons freshly grated Parmesan cheese
grated nutmeg
425 g (14 oz) fresh tagliatelle
salt and pepper

Reserve a few small asparagus tips for the garnish. Purée the remaining asparagus in a blender, or mash it with a fork. Set aside.

Melt the butter in a heavy saucepan. Add the flour and cook, stirring, for 1 minute. Gradually blend in the milk and bring it to the boil, still stirring. Simmer for 3 minutes. Stir in the asparagus purée, then the cream and Parmesan. Season with nutmeg, salt and pepper to taste. Remove from the heat.

Bring a large saucepan of salted water to the boil. Add the tagliatelle, stir and bring back to the boil. Reduce the heat and boil, uncovered, for 3-4 minutes or according to the packet instructions, stirring occasionally. Meanwhile, reheat the asparagus sauce very gently, stirring.

Drain the tagliatelle well and transfer it to a warm bowl. Add the sauce and toss the pasta well to cover it evenly with the sauce. Divide equally between 4 warm soup plates and top with the reserved asparagus tips. Serve at once with a tomato or red pepper salad and extra Parmesan handed separately.

SERVES 4

Nutritional content per serving: Carbohydrate: 36 g   Fat: 15 g   Fibre: 3 g   Kilocalories: 315

FARFALLE WITH RICOTTA AND TOMATO SAUCE

2 tablespoons olive oil
2 cloves garlic, crushed
1 × 397 g (14 oz) can chopped tomatoes with
    herbs
300 g (10 oz) dried farfalle (pasta bows)
300 g (10 oz) ricotta or curd cheese
1 tablespoon freshly grated Parmesan cheese
salt and pepper
basil sprigs to garnish

Heat the oil in a heavy saucepan. Add the garlic and fry it very gently, stirring all the time, for 1-2 minutes until it is light golden. Add the tomatoes and their juice, stir well and bring to the boil. Reduce the heat and season with salt and pepper to taste. Cover the pan and simmer for 20 minutes.

Bring a large saucepan of salted water to the boil. Add the farfalle, stir and bring back to the boil. Reduce the heat and boil, uncovered, for 8-10 minutes, or according to packet instructions, stirring occasionally.

Put the ricotta or curd cheese in a large bowl, add the grated Parmesan cheese and 3-4 tablespoons of the pasta cooking water. Beat the cheeses until they are creamy in consistency.

Drain the farfalle well. Add them to the cheese and toss well to mix them together. Divide the pasta equally between 4 warm soup plates. Taste the tomato sauce and adjust the seasoning. Pour over the pasta and garnish with basil sprigs. Serve at once.

SERVES 4

Nutritional content per serving: Carbohydrate: 66 g   Fat: 15 g   Fibre: 4 g   Kilocalories: 485

Tagliatelle with Asparagus and Cream; Farfalle with Ricotta and Tomato Sauce

Spaghetti with Saffron

SPAGHETTI WITH SAFFRON

FRESHLY GRATED PARMESAN CAN BE SERVED WITH THIS SIMPLE DISH. IT TASTES REALLY GOOD, BUT IF YOU PREFER THE SUBTLETY OF THE SAFFRON FLAVOUR IT IS BETTER TO SERVE IT WITHOUT THE CHEESE

425 g (14 oz) spaghetti
1 large pinch of saffron threads
2 tablespoons butter
½ large onion, chopped very finely
150 ml (¼ pint) extra thick double cream
salt and pepper

Bring a large saucepan of salted water to the boil. Add the spaghetti, stir and bring back to the boil. Reduce the heat and boil, uncovered, for 10-12 minutes or according to packet instructions, stirring occasionally.

Meanwhile, put the saffron threads in a heatproof bowl. Stir in 2 tablespoons of the pasta cooking water and leave the saffron to soak. Melt the butter in a heavy saucepan, add the onion and cook very gently, stirring frequently, until it is golden. Remove the pan from the heat. Strain in the saffron liquid. Pour in the cream, stirring well to blend the ingredients.

Drain the spaghetti well and turn it into a warm bowl. Reheat the saffron sauce quickly. Season with salt and pepper to taste and pour the sauce over the spaghetti, tossing it well. Serve at once.

SERVES 4

Nutritional content per serving: Carbohydrate: 86 g   Fat: 25 g   Fibre: 3 g   Kilocalories: 605

PASTA TWISTS WITH BEAN SAUCE

'MIXED BEAN SALAD' IS A COMBINATION OF GREEN, RED KIDNEY, BLACK-EYE, BORLOTTI AND CANNELLINI BEANS WITH CHICK PEAS, SWEETCORN AND RED PEPPERS

1 tablespoon olive oil

1 small onion, chopped finely

1 × 185 g (6½ oz) can pimientos (sweet red peppers), drained and sliced thinly

1 × 397 g (14 oz) can chopped tomatoes with herbs

1 × 425 g (15 oz) can mixed bean salad, drained

1 teaspoon tomato purée

375 g (12 oz) dried wholewheat pasta twists or spirals

2 tablespoons chopped parsley

salt and pepper

chervil sprigs to garnish

Heat the oil in a wok or deep, heavy frying-pan. Add the onion and stir-fry until it has softened – about 5 minutes.

Add the sliced pimientos and stir-fry for 1-2 minutes. Stir in the tomatoes with their juice, the beans and tomato purée. Season to taste. Stir well, and simmer, uncovered, for about 15 minutes.

Meanwhile, bring a large saucepan of salted water to the boil. Add the pasta twists, stir and bring back to the boil. Reduce the heat and boil, uncovered, for 10-12 minutes or according to the packet instructions, stirring occasionally.

Drain the pasta well and turn it into a warm bowl. Stir half the parsley into the bean sauce. Adjust the seasoning if necessary and pour the sauce over the pasta, tossing them together well. Divide the pasta equally between 4 warm soup plates. Scatter over the remaining parsley and serve at once. Garnish with sprigs of chervil.

SERVES 4

Nutritional content per serving: Carbohydrate: 75 g   Fat: 7 g   Fibre: 18 g   Kilocalories: 430

Pasta Twists with Bean Sauce

Macaroni, beef and sweetcorn pie

1 tablespoon olive oil

375 g (12 oz) minced beef

1 × 340 g (11½ oz) can sweetcorn and
  peppers

2 tablespoons tomato purée

2 teaspoons dried mixed herbs

250 g (8 oz) thin-cut 'quick cook' macaroni

250 g (8 oz) Quark cheese or skimmed milk
  soft cheese

1 egg

125 ml (4 fl oz) milk

pinch of grated nutmeg

125 g (4 oz) grated Mozzarella cheese

salt and pepper

Heat the oil in a heavy saucepan. Add the minced beef and cook until the meat has changed colour, stirring all the time with a wooden spoon and pressing the meat against the side of the pan to remove all lumps.

Add the sweetcorn and peppers and their liquid, the purée and herbs. Season to taste. Cook over a moderate heat for about 10 minutes until the liquid has evaporated, stirring occasionally.

Meanwhile, bring a large saucepan of salted water to the boil. Add the macaroni, stir and bring back to the boil. Reduce the heat and boil, uncovered, for 7-8 minutes or according to the packet instructions, stirring occasionally. Beat the Quark in a bowl with the egg, milk, nutmeg, salt and plenty of pepper.

Drain the macaroni well. Transfer it to a flameproof serving dish and add the beef mixture. Stir well to combine the sauce and pasta. Adjust the seasoning if necessary. Level the surface. Pour over the Quark mixture and sprinkle the grated Mozzarella on top.

Place the dish under a preheated hot grill for 8-10 minutes, or until the Mozzarella is melted and bubbling. Serve at once, straight from the dish, with a mixed salad.

Freezing: is recommended. Freeze the pie before grilling. Cover the serving dish with foil and overwrap in a freezer bag. This will keep for 1-2 months. Bake from frozen in a preheated oven 190°C, 375°F, Gas Mark 5, still with the foil covering on for 40 minutes or until bubbling and completely heated through. Remove foil to brown if necessary.

SERVES 4-6

Nutritional content per serving: Carbohydrate: 75 g   Fat: 22 g   Fibre: 7 g   Kilocalories: 625

Macaroni with mackerel and dill

375 g (12 oz) dried macaroni

1 tablespoon of lemon juice

2 cucumbers in sour-sweet vinegar, drained
  and chopped

1-2 tablespoons capers, according to taste

500 g (1 lb) smoked mackerel fillets, skinned,
boned and flaked

2 teaspoons chopped dill

200 ml (7 fl oz) mayonnaise

salt and pepper

Bring a large saucepan of salted water to the boil. Add the macaroni, stir and bring back to the boil. Reduce the heat and boil, uncovered, for 10 minutes or according to packet instructions, stirring occasionally.

Drain the macaroni well and turn it into a warm bowl. Stir in the lemon juice, cucumbers and capers, mixing the ingredients well. Carefully fold in the mackerel, the dill and plenty of pepper. Spoon the mayonnaise on top and serve at once.

SERVES 4

Nutritional content per serving: Carbohydrate: 74 g   Fat: 56 g   Fibre: 3 g   Kilocalories: 910

Macaroni, Beef and Sweetcorn Pie; Macaroni with Mackerel and Dill; Pasta, Tuna and Mushroom Bake

PASTA, TUNA AND MUSHROOM BAKE

250 g (8 oz) dried pasta shells
25 g (1 oz) butter
25 g (1 oz) plain flour
600 ml (1 pint) milk
175 g (6 oz) Double Gloucester cheese, grated
2 × 300 g (10.6 oz) cans whole button
mushrooms, drained
1 × 400 g (14 oz) can tuna, drained and
flaked
2 tablespoons chopped parsley
1 egg, beaten
salt and pepper

Bring a pan of salted water to the boil. Add the pasta, stir and bring back to the boil. Reduce the heat and boil, uncovered, for 10 minutes or according to packet instructions, stirring occasionally. Melt the butter in a heavy pan. Add the flour and cook, stirring, for 1 minute. Gradually blend in the milk. Bring it to the boil, still stirring, and simmer for 3 minutes. Remove the pan from the heat. Add about two thirds of the cheese and season to taste. Stir the sauce until the cheese has melted.

Drain the pasta well and turn it into a bowl. Fold in the mushrooms and tuna. Gently fold in about two thirds of the sauce and the parsley.

Transfer the mixture to a baking dish and level the surface. Beat the egg into the remaining cheese sauce and pour it over the top. Sprinkle over the remaining cheese. Bake in a preheated oven 190°C, 375°F, Gas Mark 5 for 20 minutes. Serve hot, straight from the dish.

SERVES 4-6

Nutritional content per serving: Carbohydrate: 65 g   Fat: 48 g   Fibre: 6 g   Kilocalories: 870

Spaghetti with mozzarella and anchovies

Nothing could be simpler than this sauce, which is made from just three ingredients, yet nothing could taste more authentically italian. If you like the flavour of garlic, it goes particularly well with mozzarella and anchovies, so you could add 1-2 crushed garlic cloves to the sauce, or even 1-2 teaspoons garlic purée

425 g (14 oz) spaghetti
2 × 50 g (2 oz) cans anchovies in oil, drained and soaked in milk for 20 minutes
1 × 250 g (8.82 oz) packet grated Mozzarella cheese
2 egg yolks
salt and pepper

Bring a large saucepan of salted water to the boil. Add the spaghetti, stir and bring back to the boil. Reduce the heat and boil, uncovered, for 10-12 minutes or according to the packet instructions, stirring occasionally.

Meanwhile, drain and dry the anchovies and chop them roughly. Place them in a large bowl with the Mozzarella cheese. Beat in the egg yolks and plenty of pepper.

Drain the spaghetti well. Transfer it to the bowl and combine it well with the cheese mixture. Divide the pasta equally between 4 warm soup plates and grind pepper over the top. Serve at once, with a plain green salad to refresh the palate.

SERVES 4

Nutritional content per serving: Carbohydrate: 84 g   Fat: 21 g   Fibre: 3 g   Kilocalories: 645

Pasta shells with pâté and cream sauce

You can vary the flavour of this deliciously creamy sauce each time you make it according to the type of pâté you choose. For a special occasion, you could use a can of pâté de foie gras. For those who like fish, use a salmon pâté

300 g (10 oz) dried pasta shells or twists
75 g (3 oz) fine, smooth liver pâté, at room temperature
1-2 teaspoons garlic purée, according to taste
4 tablespoons dry white wine (optional)
150 ml (¼ pint) single cream
1 × 300 g (10 oz) can whole button mushrooms, drained
salt and pepper
tarragon sprigs to garnish

Bring a large saucepan of salted water to the boil. Add the pasta shells, stir and bring back to the boil. Reduce the heat and boil, uncovered, for 10 minutes, or according to the packet instructions, stirring occasionally.

Meanwhile, put the pâté in a heavy saucepan with the garlic purée and the wine, if used, or 4 tablespoons of the pasta cooking water. Beat them well together. Gradually beat in all but 4 tablespoons of the cream until it is evenly incorporated. Stir in the mushrooms. Place the saucepan over a gentle heat and stir until the sauce is heated through. Season with salt and pepper to taste.

Drain the pasta well and divide equally between 4 warm soup plates. Pour over the sauce. Garnish with tarragon sprigs. Serve at once. Serve as a quick starter, with chilled dry white wine.

SERVES 4

Nutritional content per serving: Carbohydrate: 65 g   Fat: 14 g   Fibre: 4 g   Kilocalories: 440

Spaghetti with Mozzarella and Anchovies; Pasta Shells with Pâté and Cream Sauce

INDEX